WHAT IN THE WORLD!

Social Studies Projects and Activities

Susan Banfield

Interior Illustrations by: Marilyn Barr

ISBN: 0-8167-2593-4

Printed in the United States of America.

10 9 8 7 6 5 4 3 2

Contents

Introduction

A good social studies curriculum motivates children to be actively involved in the world around them. Filled with absorbing activities, **What in the World! Social Studies Projects and Activities** capitalizes on children's natural curiosity about their communities, about the lives and customs of different peoples, and about society's stories, past and present.

What in the World! Social Studies Projects and Activities is designed to supplement most standard social studies curricula for grades K–6. Its contents —suggestions for class discussions and activities, independent activities for children, and great reading for children and teachers—are clustered around nine themes commonly featured in social studies instruction: "Heroes and Holidays," "Native Americans," "From Raw Materials to Marketplace," "Communities," "Westward Expansion," "The Civil War," "Immigration," "City Life," and "Africa."

The activities in this book are fun and engrossing. With these activities, students write stories and songs, create art, and speak to their class; they report on their own communities and families; and they participate in "you are there" activities that let them imagine they are experiencing historic events and foreign places. The activities also provide background materials and reinforce skill instruction, acting in themselves as supplements to classroom learning. Map-making and map-reading activities provide small maps for students to work from or to use as models; graph-reading activities provide graphs with interesting statistics. Historical fiction and folk tales serve as models for creative writing. Because of its thematic organization, this book encourages focus. A teacher who is teaching a unit on Native Americans, for example, will find in this book a chapter full of activities on the same subject to supplement his or her core instruction.

Lastly, and perhaps most important, **What in the World! Social Studies Projects and Activities** is designed to help with the challenge of developing in students such attitudes as cooperation with peers, community involvement, and appreciation of other cultures. Many of the activities in this book have a cooperative learning approach, asking students to work together in groups. A number of them take students out into the community—to conduct interviews, visit community service organizations, and the like. Still others encourage a global perspective; these are designed to foster an awareness of the contributions and accomplishments of people of different cultures.

How the Book Is Organized

The first of the book's nine units are geared toward younger students, the later ones toward upper elementary students. Each unit begins with an introductory page that provides suggestions and resources for sparking student interest in the theme. The page contains an overview of the topic for the teacher, one or more Discussion Starters, a listing of children's trade books—including fiction—that can be used to supplement instruction, and sources of background information for the teacher that are sure to refresh his or her personal enthusiasm for the subject matter.

Each introductory page is followed by classroom activities that take a variety of different approaches to the unit theme and involve a number of different skills. Two Activity Sheets follow the classroom activities in each unit. These Activity Sheets can be photocopied, distributed to students, and worked on independently. Finally, at the end of each unit, you will find suggestions for reviewing the unit's theme with students.

Suggestions for Using the Book

Each activity in **What in the World! Social Studies Projects and Activities** is designed with both the teacher and the child in mind. It is self-contained, and includes suggestions for carrying out the project with a class. Occasionally, realia and other additional materials are required; when this is the case, the need for specific materials is always indicated. As with most effective classroom exercises, these can be used as a springboard for further learning. For example, if students feel encouraged by their success with a map-reading activity, they can create a map of their own; or when they are inspired by learning about an accomplished historical figure, they can write a monologue in which they play that person.

The completed activities are likely to have much more effect if students are encouraged to keep their work or to display it in the classroom whenever possible. Students can devote a separate section of their notebooks to saving completed activities, or set up folders or portfolios to store their work.

With many versatile activities and helpful ideas, **What in the World! Social Studies Projects and Activities** is sure to enrich students' understanding of social studies concepts, and promote genuine enjoyment of this rich and rewarding discipline.

Heroes and Holidays

Through learning about their nation's holidays, children begin to acquire a sense of national and cultural identity. At the same time, activities centered around holidays and their celebration have a natural appeal to young children, and are an ideal way for them to begin to learn something of their country's history.

A number of holidays commemorate national heroes: George Washington, Abraham Lincoln, Martin Luther King, Jr. Young children should—and can—begin to develop an appreciation of the lives of their country's great men and women. This is not just a matter of civic pride. Sociologists and educators now recognize the importance of having heroes—men and women on whom to model one's life—to a person's moral and psychological development.

DISCUSSION STARTERS

Discuss birthdays. Ask students: How are birthdays celebrated in your family? Why are birthdays important? What does a birthday celebrate? From this, build the idea that just as individuals and families have special ways to remember days that are important to them—the days on which people were born—so a nation has special ways to celebrate days that have been important in its history.

Have students name someone they would like to be like when they get older. (It could be an adult or an older child, either a real person or a fictional character.) Ask: Why would you like to be like this person? What good qualities does he or she have that you would like to have?

BIBLIOGRAPHY

FOR CHILDREN

Blackaby, Susan. **Quick and Easy Holiday Skits.** Troll, 1992.

Brandt, Keith. **George Washington.** Troll, 1985.

Conaway, Judith. **Happy Thanksgiving! Things to Make and Do.** Troll, 1986.

Matthews, Liz. **Teeny Witch and the Perfect Valentine.** Troll, 1991.

Pistolesi, Roseanna. **Let's Celebrate Christmas.** Troll, 1988.

Santrey, Laurence. **George Washington: Young Leader.** Troll, 1982.

Whitehead, Patricia. **Best Thanksgiving Book.** Troll, 1985.

FOR THE TEACHER

Bauer, Caroline Feller. **Celebrations: Read-Aloud Holiday and Theme Book Programs.** H. W. Wilson, 1985.

Making a Holiday Time Line

Begin by brainstorming a list of holidays with students. Take one season at a time. As students name holidays, write them on the chalkboard under the appropriate season. Help students by providing clues for holidays they can't think of (for example, draw an egg for Easter, a top hat for Lincoln's Birthday). Try to elicit as many of the following holidays as students are familiar with:

Lincoln's Birthday	Memorial Day	Halloween
Valentine's Day	Canada Day	Thanksgiving
Washington's Birthday	Independence Day	Hanukkah
Passover	Labor Day	Christmas
Easter	Columbus Day	

Have the children help you construct the time line. Ask for volunteers. Have children write the names of the months in dark crayon on long strips of construction paper. (Draw guidelines for writing on the strips. Adjoining months should be on strips of different colors.)

Assign each holiday named by the class to a student who did not write a month. Have each of these children copy the holiday assigned to him or her onto a large white index card. Encourage children to decorate their cards or strips.

After taping the months in calendar order to the wall, help the class tape the holiday cards above the correct months. If students do not know the month of a holiday, you can have them use a large calendar to discover it, giving clues to narrow their search. Finally, use colorful string and tape to connect each holiday to its month.

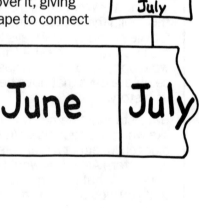

An Illustrated Life of Washington

Read to the class a simple biography of Washington, preferably one that emphasizes his boyhood. Two possible titles are *George Washington* by Keith Brandt (Troll, 1985) and *George Washington: Young Leader* by Laurence Santrey (Troll, 1982). The second pays special attention to Washington's boyhood.

Explain that you are going to make a class mural showing Washington's life in pictures. Point out that when telling the story of someone's life, you need to include all the important things that he or she did and that happened to him or her. To illustrate the concept, ask students what they think are the important events in their own lives (moves, starting school, birth of siblings, and so on). Then ask them what they think were the important events in Washington's life. List these on the chalkboard. The list might include:

- Visiting his older brother Lawrence at Mount Vernon
- His first trip as a surveyor
- Delivering a letter to the enemy during French and Indian War
- Danger in his first battle
- Winter at Valley Forge
- Surrender of the British at Yorktown
- Hearing the news that he was to be the first president of the United States

Then explain that when telling the story of someone's life it is also a good idea to include some events that are especially interesting or exciting, even if they are not the most important. Ask students which parts of Washington's life they find most interesting. List these on the chalkboard as they are mentioned, exploring them further in discussion. (What made it interesting or exciting? What did you like about it?)

Assign each event on the board to a small group of students, and have each group draw a picture to illustrate the event. Help the class to arrange the illustrations in the correct time sequence on a bulletin board. Provide simple captions.

GEORGE WASHINGTON CROSSING THE DELAWARE 1776

"We Shall Overcome"

Read to the class a brief biography of Martin Luther King, Jr. One possible title is *Martin Luther King* by Rae Bains (Troll, 1985). Explain that we can often learn lessons from how other people lived their lives—lessons about what to do or what not to do when we have a certain kind of problem. Explain that many people have learned valuable lessons from the life of Martin Luther King, Jr. For example, people have learned from Dr. King's battle against social injustice that they can overcome even very serious difficulties that face them as long as they have patience and courage and are willing to work hard. People of all races and backgrounds have learned from Dr. King's story.

Discuss other difficult problems that different people face in their lives. (Try to steer the discussion away from topics that are too personal.)

Reporting on Famous American Women

Present a simple format for writing a book report. Then have students read a biography of a famous American woman and do a book report on it.

One possible format is:

1. Name of book
2. Name of author
3. Who this book is about
4. What this person did that other women of her time did not do
5. What young people today can learn from this person's life
6. Special lessons I learned from her life
7. What I liked best about this book
8. What I liked least about it

The Troll Easy Biographies Library (for grades 4–6) contains biographies of many famous American women, including:

Louisa May Alcott   Helen Keller
Clara Barton   Eleanor Roosevelt
Elizabeth Blackwell   Harriet Tubman
Amelia Earhart   Narcissa Whitman

Invite students to present their reports orally as well as in writing. After all of your students have given their reports, ask them which woman they would like to read about next, and why.

What We Are Thankful For

Give students an opportunity to express their gratitude visually, in conjunction with the celebration of Thanksgiving.

First, review the story of the first Thanksgiving. Ask: What were the Pilgrims thankful for? (Answers can include: having survived a winter, their first harvest, the help of their Native-American friends.)

Then ask students what in their lives today they are thankful for. Elicit as many answers as possible, and write them all on the chalkboard.

Prepare several large patterns of a cornucopia. Use this as a template to cut cornucopias out of large pieces of construction paper, one for each student.

Then have the students cut pictures of some of the things they are thankful for out of old magazines. They can add labels to symbolic pictures to make their meaning clear. They should paste these down at the opening of the cornucopia.

The cornucopias can be labeled ''(Name) is thankful for . . .'' and taped up around the classroom.

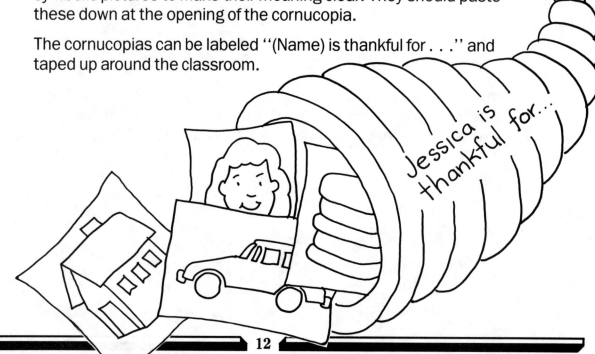

Jessica is thankful for...

Planning a Canada Day Parade

Review with the class why Canada Day (July 1) is celebrated. Be sure students understand that July 1, 1867 was the day on which Quebec, Ontario, New Brunswick, and Nova Scotia were first joined into the Dominion of Canada. (For this reason, Canada Day was originally known as Dominion Day.) This was the beginning of modern, united Canada.

Many communities have parades to celebrate Canada Day. Explain that in a parade, the marchers include representatives of all the departments and organizations that help to run a town. Sometimes the armed forces march too. Plan a Canada Day parade as a class.

First, brainstorm a list of all the groups that students would invite to march in the parade, keeping in mind the above criteria. You may also want to have students decide what order the groups will march in.

Next, have students show the route on a map of your town or city. Make photocopies of a map that is simple enough for young children to read. (You may want to blow up just one area of the city.) Read aloud a simple route for a parade, having children follow along with a pencil on their maps. Include at least one right-hand and one left-hand turn, and be sure the parade route passes historic buildings and monuments.

Holiday Traditions

Draw a line from the holiday to the picture that shows something special used on that day.

1. New Year's Eve   a.

2. Valentine's Day   b.

3. Easter   c.

4. Passover   d.

5. Memorial Day   e.

6. Independence Day   f.

7. Halloween   g.

8. Thanksgiving   h.

9. Hanukkah   i.

10. Christmas   j.

Reading Kate's Calendar

FEBRUARY						
SUN	MON	TUES	WED	THURS	FRI	SAT
1	2	3	4	5	6	7 Bobby's birthday party!
8	9	10	11	12	13	14 Valentine's Day
15	16 Presidents' Day	17	18	19	20	21
		SCHOOL VACATION →				
22	23	24	25	26	27	28

1. What day of the week is Valentine's Day? _____

2. What is the date of Valentine's Day? _____

3. What day of the week is Presidents' Day? _____

4. What is the date of Presidents' Day? _____

5. What is Kate doing on February 7? _____

Reviewing Heroes and Holidays

One Holiday, Many Traditions

Choose a holiday that everyone in the class celebrates, such as Thanksgiving. Have each student tell how his or her family celebrates the holiday: special foods served, decorations, going to a particular person's house, prayers or religious services. Write all the different traditions on the chalkboard. Emphasize how different traditions can all bring out the theme of the holiday. Then have the class make up several new traditions for the holiday you have selected.

Unsung Heroes and Heroines

Discuss how having heroes to look up to and emulate helps us to grow up to be better people. Nearly everyone has heroes, although they may not be famous. Sometimes a relative or a teacher or an older boy or girl in the neighborhood can be a hero.

Have each student name someone who is a hero to him or her. It might be someone famous—the president, a sports figure, or a television personality—or an "unsung hero" such as those mentioned above. Then make a tally on the chalkboard. See which heroes come up most often.

Teaching children about the ways of the first Americans is an important part of building respect and understanding for these special groups. It is also an ideal way to introduce students to several important social studies concepts, including:

- How people's lives are determined by the resources that are available to them
- The many ways people make use of the resources they find around them

A teacher can take any number of different approaches to these topics, from informational to problem-solving to hands-on activities.

DISCUSSION STARTER

Native Americans use natural resources wisely. To demonstrate this point, list the items on the left on the chalkboard. Then have students try to think what Native Americans of the Northwest Coast have used to make these things. After students have guessed, write the correct answers on the right, on the chalkboard.

bows	yew tree
harpoons	yew tree
bowls	yellow cedar and alder
dishes	yellow cedar and alder
spoons	yellow cedar and alder
houses	red cedar
canoes	red cedar
totem poles	red cedar
boxes	red cedar
masks	red cedar
skirts	cedar bark, woven
capes	cedar bark, woven
rain hats	cedar bark
dolls	cedar

Help students to see how ingenious these Native Americans have been in using their most plentiful resource—trees—wisely and respectfully, by making ceremonial art and reusable items.

BIBLIOGRAPHY

FOR CHILDREN
Bains, Rae. **Indians of the Eastern Woodlands.** Troll, 1985.

Brandt, Keith. **Indian Homes.** Troll, 1985.

Jassem, Kate. **Sacajawea: Wilderness Guide.** Troll, 1979.

Jeffers, Susan. **Brother Eagle, Sister Sky.** Dial, 1991.

Moser, Barry. **And Still the Turtle Watched.** Dutton, 1991.

FOR THE TEACHER
Brown, Dee. **Bury My Heart at Wounded Knee.** Holt, 1971.

Caduto, Michael J., and Bruchac, Joseph. **Keepers of the Earth: Native American Stories and Environmental Activities for Children.** Fulcrum, 1989.

Wilbur, C. Keith. **Indian Handcrafts.** Globe Pequot, 1990.

W here Native Americans Lived

Create a classroom mural showing where the different groups of Native Americans originally lived. Obtain a large inexpensive map of North America or the United States. Use a broad, dark marker to mark off the areas as shown on the map below. Prepare large labels for the different major areas. You will probably also want to prepare smaller labels, on paper of different colors, for the principal groups in each area (a partial list is given below).

Explain to students that the different areas on the map are named either for their location (Northwest Coast, Southwest, California), topographical features (Woodlands, Plains, Basin-Plateau), or climate (Subarctic, Arctic). Encourage students to decorate the areas with the appropriate topographical features and label the areas. Then have them add labels for the names of the Native-American groups that lived in each area.

You may also wish to have the children make small pictures of the homes, clothing, common articles, or everyday activities of the different Native American groups. You can guide them in using library books as resources.

Northwest Coast	Basin-Plateau	Plains	Southwest
Chinook	Shoshone	Cheyenne	Navajo
Kwakiutl	Nez Percé	Sioux	Pueblo
Haida	Ute	Blackfeet	Apache
Nootka	Paiute	Comanche	

──────── Woodlands ────────

Northeast	Southeast	California	Subarctic
Iroquois	Seminole	Pomo	Algonquin
Mohegan	Cherokee	Hupa	Chipewyan
Delaware	Choctaw	Yokut	Tanaina
Susquehanna	Creek		Yellowknife

Arctic
Inuit

Silent Speech: Native American Sign Language

Explain that the Native American groups of the Plains region spoke many different languages. The different groups developed a universal way of talking with their hands, so that they could all communicate without words.

I/me

see

hear: turn your hand backward and forward slightly by moving your wrist

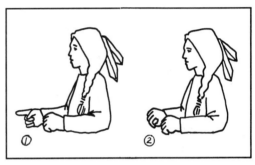

afraid: when making the first sign, point to whatever you are afraid of with your right index finger

fast: pass right hand quickly over left, then touch left palm with right fingertips

love/friend: lift your hand until your fingertips reach the level of your chin

cat: move your right hand slowly away from your face, with your fingers in the same position; then show the size of the cat with your two hands

horse: raise your right palm in front of the left side of your chest

wolf: move your hand on a slant in front of you, keeping your two fingers extended

Write some simple sentences on the chalkboard, such as:

I see a fast horse.

The cat is afraid of the wolf.

Have students "translate" these into sign language.

Making a Kwakiutl Mask

The Kwakiutl people of the Northwest Coast region were known for their carved wooden masks, which they wore at elaborate celebrations called potlatches. Show students pictures of these masks:

Kwakiutl masks

Help pupils to make masks out of papier-mâché. First, assemble the needed materials: a bucket, white wood glue, brushes, water, old newspapers (some cut into 1-inch [2½-cm] strips, others left as is), poster paints in bright colors. Mix paste by combining equal parts of warm water and glue.

Help each student make a base for his or her mask by crumpling up paper about the size and shape of a face. Then demonstrate how to dip the first strips in the paste and place them smoothly on the base. Let each layer dry somewhat before going on to the next layer. Subsequent layers are formed by "painting" paste on with a brush and then putting on strips. Students can make a nose by crumpling up a small bit of paper and covering it with coated strips. When a relatively smooth surface has been achieved, let masks dry thoroughly.

Students can then paint the masks with poster paint and pull the crumpled paper base out of the back. To give their masks a distinctively Kwakiutl look, suggest they paint thick bold lines in bright colors on their masks. Point out that the Kwakiutl often made masks that looked like wild animals.

Native Americans: Many Different Peoples

Construct a chart to help students see how very different the life-styles of the various Native American peoples originally were. Help them to see that most of these differences were the result of the kinds of resources that groups in various parts of the continent had on hand.

Construct a chart such as the one below. Allow students to choose which groups they will look up. Let them use books on the various groups, such as those mentioned in the introduction to the Native Americans section, or have them use an encyclopedia. Assign several students to work together on each group.

	Resources	Home	Clothing	Food	Special Crafts
Plains groups	buffalo, grass	earth lodges	made of buffalo hide	buffalo, corn, beans, squash	feathered beadwork

After the chart has been completed, help students to see the connection between what is listed in the Resources column and what is listed in the other four columns.

Listen to a Legend

Many Native Americans are great storytellers. There are numerous Native American tales and legends that children enjoy listening to. Native American Legends, a series published by Watermill Press in 1990, contains six books written and adapted by Terri Cohlene and illustrated by Charles Reasoner:

Quillworker: A Cheyenne Legend
Little Firefly: An Algonquian Legend
Dancing Drum: A Cherokee Legend

Turquoise Boy: A Navajo Legend
Ka-ha-si and the Loon:
   An Eskimo Legend
Clamshell Boy: A Makah Legend

Read the legends aloud to the class. In addition, you may want to read aloud "Fire," a story of the Alabama Indians, below.

Fire

Many, many years ago, men and women did not have fires to keep themselves warm or to cook with. All the fire in the world belonged to the bears. The bears guarded Fire closely. They took it with them when they hunted for wild berries, when they played with their cubs, when they bathed—wherever they went.

One day the bears were careless with Fire. They had found some delicious acorns in the forest. They set Fire on the ground while they ate. The acorns were so good that they wandered off looking for more of them, and forgot Fire. Fire almost went out.

"Feed me!" Fire cried. But the bears did not hear.

A man happened to see Fire flickering and sputtering weakly. He picked up four sticks and laid them on top of Fire. Fire roared and sent its flames shooting high in the air. It lit up the dark grove of the forest with its huge blaze and made the man toasty warm.

When the bears returned from their acorn hunt and looked for Fire, Fire sneered at them: "I don't even know you." It sent up great shooting flames so hot that the bears could not come near it.

The bears never got Fire back. Now Fire belongs to men and women.

A Day in the Lives of Native Americans

Choose one Native American group, preferably one on which a lot of pictorial material is available, and have the class make a mural depicting early daily life for that group. A useful organizational device is that of having the mural show a typical day in the life of a boy and a girl (or young man and young woman) of the group.

Help students to brainstorm everything they will want in the mural. They may wish to show the inside and outside of a home; people gathering food by hunting, farming, gathering, or fishing; people engaged in other daily activities; and a ritual in which traditional dress is worn. You may want to list students' ideas on the chalkboard before they begin working on the mural.

Each topic might be assigned to a small group of students. Help groups of students to use the books you have made available, so that they can find the pictures and information they need.

Once students have gathered their information, they may want to come together and devise a simple story line, with two main characters, around which to organize the mural. With or without a story, students should then work in their groups to make pictures illustrating their topics. The papers can then be taped or tacked together to form a mural.

Answers to "Nakuti Goes Visiting," page 24: **1.** west **2.** north, west **3.** west, north **4.** east **5.** south

Name _____ Date _____

Nakuti Goes Visiting

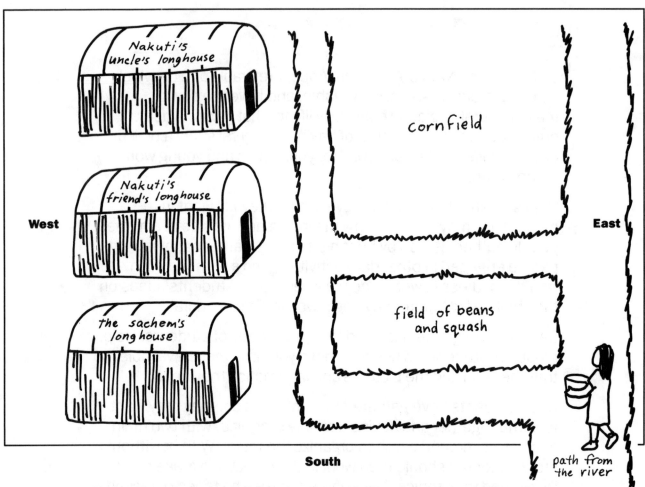

Nakuti has just come from the river. He has been given directions to three longhouses in the village. Write *north*, *south*, *east*, or *west* to complete the directions.

1. To the *sachem's longhouse:* Turn and head _____ on the path just before the field of beans and squash.

2. To *Nakuti's friend's longhouse:* Keep walking _____ on the path from the river. Turn and head _____ on the path between the cornfield and the field of beans and squash.

3. To *Nakuti's uncle's longhouse:* Head _____ on the path just before the field of beans and squash. Then turn and head _____ when

you come to the sachem's longhouse. When you come to the cornfield, your uncle's longhouse will be on the left.

Now write direction words to complete these sentences.

4. The cornfield is _____ of Nakuti's uncle's longhouse.

5. The sachem's longhouse is _____ of Nakuti's friend's longhouse.

Coloring a Sand Painting

Follow the directions to color in the sand painting.

1. Color the two bears brown. (The bears are in the lower left and upper right corners.)

2. Color the butterfly on the left red.

3. Color the butterfly on the right orange.

4. Color the snake in the top left corner black.

5. Color the snake in the bottom right corner blue.

6. Color the tall grass yellow.

7. Finish coloring the rest of the sand painting any way you would like.

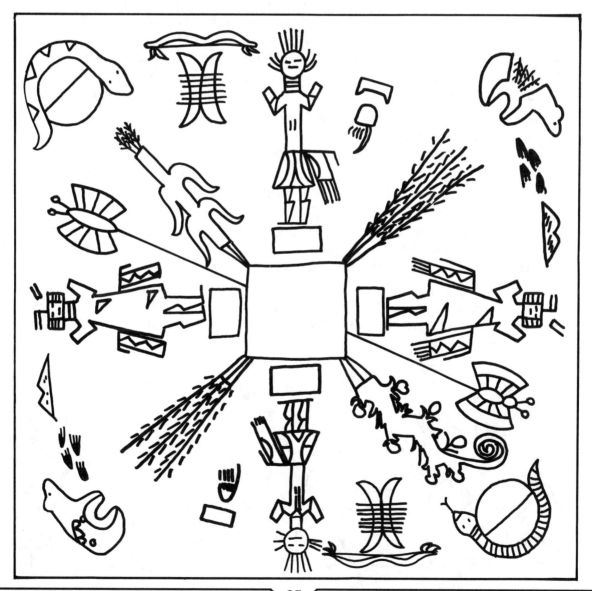

25

Reviewing Native Americans

Help students to see how Native Americans were clever at solving the problems posed by their environment. Then give students an opportunity to try solving similar problems.

1. The Native Americans who lived in the northeast Woodlands region found that their corn did not grow well in the sandy soil near the coast. What was the problem? What did they do to make the corn grow better? (Answer: They used fish to fertilize it.)

2. You are growing a houseplant in a pot on the kitchen table. It is not doing well. What might the problem be? (Possible answers: lack of sunlight, not enough water, too much water, needs fertilizer.) What might you do to make your plant healthier? (Possible answers: Move it into the sun, water it more, water it less, fertilize it.)

3. The Native Americans who lived in the Plains region had very few trees available from which to make houses. What kind of house did they make instead? (Answer: They made tepees by covering a frame of branches with buffalo hides.)

4. Wood is still scarce in the area where the Plains people lived. What can people do today to build houses that the Plains people could not do a century ago? (Possible answers: Ship in wood from elsewhere, use brick or stone.)

5. The Native Americans who settled in the Southwest region lived on land that received very little rain. How did they manage to farm and raise crops? (Answer: They dug ditches to bring water from nearby streams.)

6. Almost anyplace in the country can have a time when there is not enough rain to grow crops. What could you do to save water at such a time? (Possible answers: Take fewer showers and baths, water the lawn less, fix leaky faucets, wash the car less often, don't leave water running.)

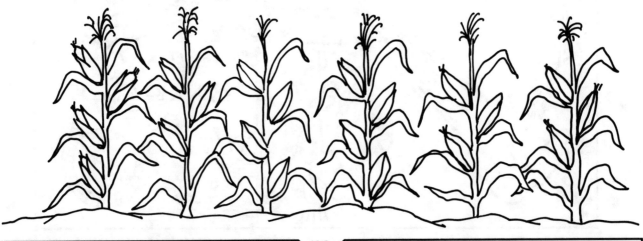

From Raw Materials to Marketplace

Even young children can grasp basic concepts of economics. They can understand that finished products are made from raw materials and that goods must often be transported from where they are made to where people want to buy them. In fact, children are often very curious to learn how things are made and where things come from. With young children, it is best to stick to concrete examples and avoid abstract economic concepts. Fortunately, there are many simple manufacturing processes that are easily accessible and of interest to young learners.

DISCUSSION STARTERS

Ask students: What did you have for breakfast this morning? Help students to trace the items to the different stores where their families shop, then trace the items to where they were grown or made. Explain that the oranges in the orange juice may have come from California or Florida, that the corn in the corn flakes may have been grown in Iowa, and so on. Show these places on a map of the United States.

Show students an ear of corn and a bowl of corn flakes. Ask: How do you think the corn flakes were made from corn? Help students to specify as many steps in the process as possible: shucking the corn, scraping off the kernels and drying them, grinding the corn, adding other ingredients to make a batter, and baking the flakes.

BIBLIOGRAPHY

FOR CHILDREN
Aliki. **How a Book Is Made.** Harper, 1988.

Ancona, George, and Anderson, Joan. **The American Family Farm.** Harcourt, 1989.

Corey, Melinda. **Let's Visit a Spaghetti Factory.** Troll, 1990.

Locker, Thomas. **Family Farm.** Dial, 1988.

O'Neill, Catherine. **Let's Visit a Chocolate Factory.** Troll, 1988.

Poskanzer, Susan Cornell. **What's It Like To Be a Dairy Farmer.** Troll, 1989.

Ziefert, Harriet. **A New Coat for Anna.** Knopf, 1986.

FOR THE TEACHER
Clarke, Donald, ed. **The Encyclopedia of How It's Made.** A&W, 1978.

Gottlieb, Leonard. **Factory Made: How Things Are Manufactured.** Houghton Mifflin, 1978.

Hamper, Ben. **Rivethead.** Warner, 1991.

Kidder, Tracy. **The Soul of a New Machine.** Little, Brown, 1981.

Homemade Butter

Ask students if they know where butter comes from. Establish that it is made from milk. Ask if anyone knows how butter is made from milk. Allow students to brainstorm different ideas. Then explain the process as follows: There is a lot of fat in milk. The part that contains the fat rises to the top, since fat is lighter than water. This fatty part of the milk is called cream. The fat can be separated out of the cream if it is beaten vigorously. During the beating, the most solid fat—which is butter—separates from the liquid.

Have students work in groups to make butter. Provide each group of three or four children with a large bowl and a small bowl, an eggbeater, a slotted spoon, a small spoon, and whipping cream. Let them take turns beating until the butter separates out. Have them use a slotted spoon to remove the butter to a small bowl, then a small spoon to mix in a little salt. Provide bread or plain crackers for the students to spread their butter on and sample.

It's Made Right in My Hometown!

Take the class on a field trip to a local factory. Prepare the class by discussing beforehand the different steps in the manufacturing process:

- What raw materials are used
- Where the raw materials come from and how they are transported to the factory
- The various steps in the manufacturing process—which are done by machine and which are done by people
- How the finished goods are packaged
- Where the goods are shipped, and how
- How the finished product is used by the consumer

When your class visits the factory, make sure the children see the raw materials and, if possible, the trucks on which they were shipped, to give them an idea of the distance these materials may have traveled. You may also wish to interview someone who is in charge of shipping at the factory. After viewing the steps of the manufacturing process, again try to have children see finished goods being readied for shipping and loaded onto trucks. If possible, arrange for students to be given some sort of sample to take away with them.

Have students summarize the experience by writing a paragraph in which they explain, in proper sequence, how the item they have seen is made. For very young children you may write the actual sentences on the chalkboard in a scrambled order, then have children rearrange them in the correct order.

Assembly Line Production

Give students an opportunity to experience making a simple object—a shoe-box "wagon"—on an assembly line. Have on hand the following supplies: wire hangers (one per student), shoe boxes (one per student), 3-inch ($7\frac{1}{2}$-cm) square jewelry boxes (two per student), small thread spools (four per student), strong tape (several rolls). Have wire cutters and pliers on hand for yourself and other participating adults.

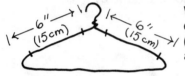

With a pair of wire cutters, cut out of hanger two 6-inch (15-cm) lengths of wire for axles, and one handle.

Straighten handle of hanger to make wagon handle.

Divide students into groups of four. Set up assembly line stations and provide each assembly line with enough materials to produce one cart per worker.

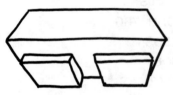

Group 1: Tape two jewelry boxes to bottom of a shoe box.

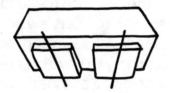

Group 2: Tape wire axles across jewelry boxes.

Group 3: Slip spools onto axles.

Help students by using pliers to turn up ends of axles.

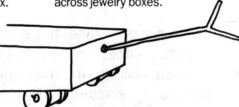

Group 4: Pierce front of box with straightened coat hanger "handle."

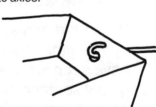

Help students by using pliers to bend back end of handle inside box to secure.

After all carts have been produced, discuss the pros and cons of assembly line production. Did students like the assembly line method, or would they have preferred to make their own cart from start to finish?

Petroleum: "Black Gold"

Help children to make a bulletin-board display of the many different products derived from petroleum, or oil. Some to include are cosmetics, hair-care products, alcohol, paint, asphalt, plastics, and medicines, in addition to the more familiar products such as motor oil, heating oil, and gasoline. Invite children to clip pictures from magazines or bring in labels from common household items made from petroleum. Have children discuss why it is often referred to as "black gold."

ITEMS MADE FROM PETROLEUM

From Poplar to Paper

Help students to understand how a common product such as paper is made from raw materials. Steps to explain should include the following:

- Gathering logs from a wood yard
- Removing the logs' bark
- Cutting the logs into chips and washing them
- Breaking down the chips into individual fibers, often done by using chemicals
- Washing the broken-down pulp and removing imperfections
- Squeezing out the water and forming the refined pulp into sheets, by means of a series of rollers

Have students make a simple flow chart of the process, by making a picture of each step and connecting these pictures with arrows that indicate the direction of the process.

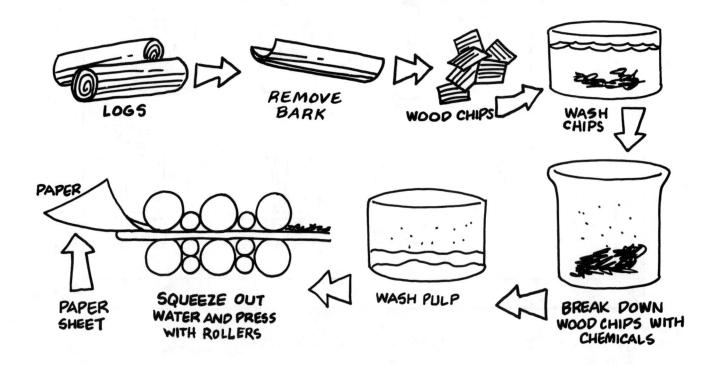

Making a Simple Product Map

Ask students: If there were three spots in your backyard where different kinds of weeds grew easily, how would you show those places on a map? Encourage a variety of responses, but build on those that approach the idea of using symbols.

Brainstorm with the class some of the products of your state. Ask if students know where in the state these items are made or grown.

Next, have students develop symbols for each item on the list (don't use too many). They may work individually or in pairs or groups. Be sure to list the symbols in a key on the completed map.

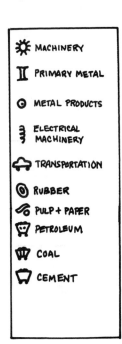

Trace a large outline map of your state. Help students to make their symbols out of construction paper. These can be glued or tacked in place in the appropriate spot.

Answers to "What Is It Made Of?", page 35: **1.** d **2.** e **3.** i **4.** h **5.** g **6.** f **7.** a. **8.** b **9.** c

An International Shopping List

The items on this list can all be found at the supermarket—but they are often imported from other countries around the world. To find out where the items on this list come from, go to the supermarket with an adult. Read the labels on these products, or ask the grocer. If you can't find out at the store, an almanac will tell you.

In the blank next to each item, write the name of at least one country that produces it. If the country you live in produces the item, include your country and at least one other country.

cocoa _____   rice _____

_____   _____

sugar _____   fish _____

_____   _____

bananas _____   pharmaceuticals _____

_____   _____

olive oil _____   beef _____

_____   _____

tobacco _____   tea _____

_____   _____

coffee _____   cheese _____

_____   _____

oranges _____

_____

What Is It Made Of?

Draw a line from each item on the left to what it is made of or where it is from.

1.

2.

3.

4.

5.

6.

7.

8.

9.

a.

b.

c.

d.

e.

f.

g.

h.

i.

Reviewing From Raw Materials to Marketplace: Home Factory

Have students present oral reports, perhaps in a show-and-tell format, about items that people make at home with their families. Have them tell about the following:

- What materials and tools are used to make the finished product
- What are the steps, in order, in making the item

Some possible items include: different foods, wooden items, sewn items, knitted items, and vegetables grown in a garden.

Divide the class into several groups. Give each group one of each of the following items, or something similar:

    shoe box
    clothespins
    pipe cleaners
    macaroni
    paper bag
    empty cylindrical oatmeal container

Give the groups ten minutes to come up with as many items as possible that they could "manufacture" with their "raw materials." Tell students they can use additional materials in their manufacturing process (glue, string, and so on).

Communities

All communities, from the largest cities to the smallest rural towns, have a number of common characteristics. They are made up of people who have divided up responsibility for providing necessities and thus depend on one another for goods and services. The members of a community choose to establish laws for the good of everyone. And in order to make systems of labor, law, and government work, communities need ways to transport people or products from one place to another—and ways for residents to communicate.

Students can begin to develop an understanding of communities at a young age. This understanding can be steadily deepened as they grow. Older students can appreciate the work done by many different types of service workers in communities, from police officers, sanitation workers, and fire fighters to those who work with the elderly or maintain local parks. Students should ultimately develop an awareness of the many different needs and wants community workers provide. Their basic understanding of rules and laws can be expanded to include a knowledge of how their own community is governed and what specific institutions are found there. Students can also learn how citizens can recognize and work together to accomplish a needed change in their community and how citizens can use means of communication such as the local newspaper or radio. Students can also begin to develop a sense of civic pride. This sense of pride is a natural result of becoming involved in one's community and of learning about its history and current affairs.

DISCUSSION STARTERS

Ask your students: Who serves people in your community? How do they help? Encourage as many different answers as possible. Then ask: Who in your neighborhood/on your block/on your street serves people in your community? As students answer, help them to see that even ordinary people help the community in many ways. Finally, ask: How do you and your family serve the community?

BIBLIOGRAPHY

FOR CHILDREN

Gibbons, Gail. **Department Store.** Harper, 1986.

Knowlton, Jack. **Books and Libraries.** Harper, 1991.

Matthews, Morgan. **What's It Like to Be a Postal Worker.** Troll, 1990.

"Our Town" (board game) by Aristoplay, 1989.

Pellowski, Michael J. **What's It Like to Be a Fire Fighter.** Troll, 1989.

Poskanzer, Susan Cornell. **What's It Like to Be a Sanitation Worker.** Troll, 1989.

Von Tscharner, Renata, and Fleming, Ronald L. **New Providence: A Changing Cityscape.** Gulliver, 1987.

FOR THE TEACHER

Gans, Herbert. **The Levittowners: Ways of Life and Politics in a New Suburban Community.** Columbia University Press, 1982.

League of Women Voters materials, available from your local branch, have information about how your community is run.

Our Town's History at a Glance

Help the class to make a time line of your town's history. Your local historical society or the local library can provide you with materials that give important events and dates.

Begin by listing as a class the major dates and events from American history in general: the coming of the Pilgrims, the American Revolution, the Civil War, the freeing of African Americans, the two World Wars, the Great Depression, and so on. Decide which of these affected your town and should be put on your time line.

Then divide the class into groups. Have each group take one era to focus on. If available materials on local history are at an appropriate reading level, have the students themselves make a list of important events and dates from their period. If the reading level is too high, provide help by reading sections aloud to students and asking whether they think each is important enough to include on the time line.

Once each group has completed their small time line, help students to make and label a large time line. A long roll of shelf paper is useful for this purpose. Students may want to illustrate the time line by drawing scenes from your town's history.

1700 — OUR FIRST SETTLERS

1775 — OUR PART IN THE REVOLUTIONARY WAR

1922 — FLAPPERS AT A BENEFIT DANCE

Inquiring Local Reporter

Tell the class to find out more about the people who serve their community by interviewing those people.

First, as a class, brainstorm a list of the many different people who serve your town or city. Encourage students to interpret this concept broadly; don't limit the list to fire fighters, police officers, and other traditional community workers.

Next, have each student choose one person from the list to interview.

Prepare students for the interviews by helping them to develop questions to ask. Possible questions might include the following: How did you get interested in your line of work? How long have you been doing this? How long have you been working for this town/city? What do you find most rewarding about your work? What can residents of the town/city do to help make your work easier?

You may also want to review the etiquette and mechanics of conducting an interview:

- Set up an appointment in advance and keep it.
- Come prepared with a list of intelligent questions and other items such as pencil and paper and a tape recorder (if available).
- Take enough notes to remember what has been said, but not so many that it slows the interview.
- Write a thank-you note afterward.

Give students an opportunity to present the results of their interviews to the class. Point out the importance of conveying accurate information in discussing interviews.

Visiting the Seat of Local Government

Take the class on a field trip to your local Town Hall, Borough Hall, or City Hall. Before making the trip, teach students about the various individuals and groups that govern the town and what role each plays in running the community. Be sure they are familiar with whichever of the following terms are appropriate for your town or city: mayor, selectman, town council, board of aldermen, city council.

To provide a focus for your visit, select a problem with which your community has been wrestling lately—perhaps a need to cut the city budget, or a controversy over whether a new development will be permitted. Help students to learn about the issue and what has been done about it to date. Local newspapers are ideal for this. While visiting your local government headquarters, have students find out exactly what role each person or chamber you visit has played in dealing with the issue.

On the visit, talk to employees with many different positions and titles. Invite these people to tell what they do to see that the town or city's business is conducted smoothly.

Have students make graphic organizers of the information they gather on the trip. A sample graphic organizer is shown below.

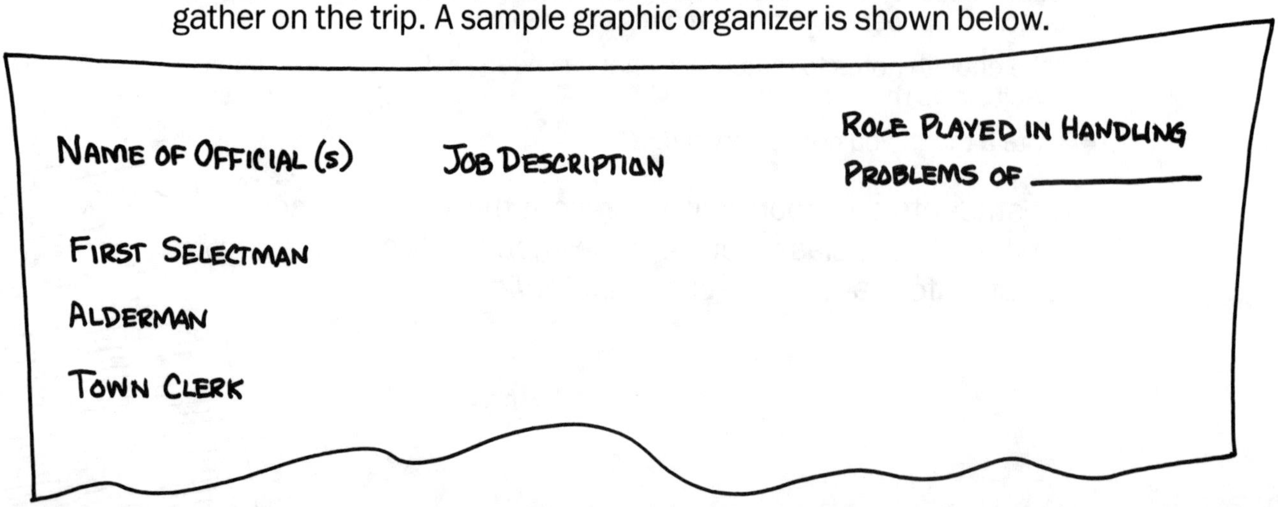

NAME OF OFFICIAL(S)   JOB DESCRIPTION   ROLE PLAYED IN HANDLING PROBLEMS OF _____

FIRST SELECTMAN

ALDERMAN

TOWN CLERK

Getting People to Help

Discuss the many ways ordinary citizens can help make their community a better place to live, such as not littering, not making noise late at night, conserving water, recycling, obeying the speed limit, and driving carefully. Discuss ways to build enthusiasm for such measures: radio campaigns, articles in the local paper, posters. Discuss the effectiveness of a poster campaign. Perhaps students have seen a particular event well publicized by posters all over town and remember the impact these posters had on them.

As a class, mount a small poster campaign to encourage one of the actions mentioned above. Have each student design and execute a poster. Decide on strategic locations to place the posters and secure permission to display them. You may also want to have a local reporter do a small story on the campaign as a way of garnering additional publicity.

Letter to the Editor

Have students write letters to the editor of your local newspaper on the issue selected on the preceding page.

As students work on their letters, help them to focus on supporting their arguments with facts and examples. Help them first to state each argument clearly in a sentence. Then discuss ways to support the argument with examples, especially from their own experience, and facts. You may want to have some books, pamphlets, or articles available for students to use as sources. Have each student use an outline such as the one shown below to plan and develop each argument.

Argument _____

_____

Supporting Example _____

_____

Supporting Example _____

_____

Fact 1 in Support _____

Fact 2 in Support _____

Also remind students of the importance of including a strong introductory and concluding statement. You may wish to review with them the proper form for writing a business letter. Encourage students to send their letters to the local newspaper. Then follow up by displaying any published letters on the class bulletin board.

B e a Mapmaker

Have students make a map of part of their community—their neighborhood, the downtown area, the area around the school, or some other area they know well. To develop students' visual skills, encourage them to walk the area they are mapping and make a sketch on the spot, rather than simply work from memory. Although the students cannot be expected to do an accurate rendering of scale, encourage them to represent proportions and relative lengths and distances as closely as they can. Discuss the importance of an accurate map, and remind students how frustrating it is when someone gives them directions or draws them a map that is incorrect.

Have them show all important landmarks, inventing symbols for such stock items as churches, schools, hospitals, and parks. Be sure they explain these symbols in a map key.

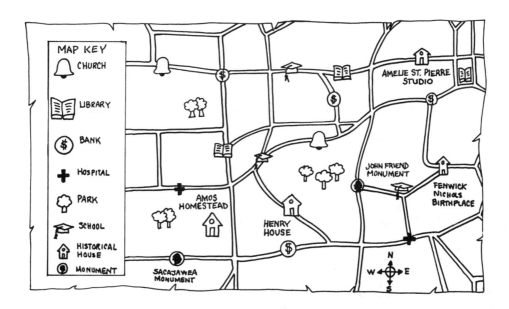

Answers to "Using a Topographical Map," page 44: **1.** 260 feet (79m) above sea level **2.** 80-120 feet (24-37m) **3.** the stores, the churches, and the school
4. the lines for the different elevations are very close together **5.** the hill on the left side is too steep

Using a Topographical Map

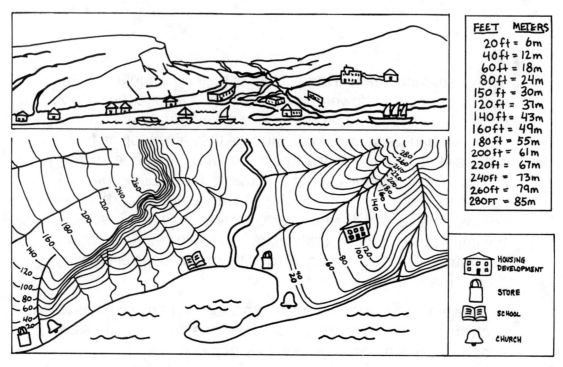

NUMBERS REPRESENT NO. OF FEET (METERS) ABOVE SEA LEVEL

Compare the drawing and the map above. Then answer the questions.

1. How high is the hill on the left? _____

2. How far above sea level is the housing development? _____

3. What buildings are built at sea level? _____

   _____

4. Describe how a steep hill is shown on a topographical map. _____

   _____

5. Why do you think the housing development was built on the hill on the right side of the valley, rather than on the hill on the left side? _____

   _____

Using a Directory of Local Services

The sample directory of community services is similar to those found in most telephone books. The numbers shown are make-believe. Use the directory to write a telephone number to call for help with each problem listed below.

ALCOHOL AND DRUG PROBLEMS

Alateen 555-9080
Alcoholics Anonymous 555-7612
Cocaine Hotline 555-5555

CHILDREN

Missing Children Hotline 555-7777
Dept. of Youth Services 555-9119

CONSUMER SERVICES

Dept. of Consumer Protection 555-5993
Credit Counseling 555-2000

FOOD

Food Stamps Information 555-0080
Overeaters Anonymous 555-8035

HEALTH INFORMATION

AIDS Hotline 555-0020
American Red Cross 555-6524
Cancer Society 555-8702

LEGAL SERVICES

Legal Aid 555-1123

POISON CONTROL

Poison Control Center 555-8000

SERVICES FOR THE ELDERLY

Dept. on Aging 555-4422
Meals on Wheels 555-0021
Medicaid 555-6655
Senior Center 555-5678

TRANSPORTATION

Bus Information 555-8990
Car Pool Assistance 555-4289

1. You are writing a paper on alcoholism. _____

2. You think your little sister ate lead paint. _____

3. You want to know more about AIDS. _____

4. You aren't sure what items you can buy with food stamps. _____

5. Your mother wants to find someone to ride to work with. _____

6. A store won't replace a defective toaster you bought. _____

7. Your elderly neighbor will need someone to bring him his meals. _____

Reviewing Communities

Have students make fact sheets for their town or city. As a class, brainstorm types of facts people most often want to know about a particular place. The facts might include the following:

- Population, perhaps with breakdown by age or ethnic group
- Area in square miles
- Neighboring towns
- Date founded
- Major industries
- Important buildings
- Schools

Also brainstorm unusual facts some people might be interested in knowing:

- Number of pizza parlors
- Number of streets named after a person
- Number of local Girl and/or Boy Scout troops

Sources for this sort of information can usually be obtained from the local Chamber of Commerce.

Have students present their information on large sheets of construction paper. They may want to decorate these with pictures—either drawings or photographs—of their community.

BAYVILLE, U.S.A.

Population: 30,000

Founded: 1888

Major Industries: Paper Electronics

Number of Pizza Parlors: 30 !!

Westward Expansion

Children are intrigued to learn about the days of America's westward expansion. They love to hear the stories about the pioneering men and women who helped settle the western states through their rugged individualism, resourcefulness, and courage. The many tales of adventure from this era are among the most thrilling and enjoyable stories in American literature.

Children's natural attraction to the subject provides a good opportunity to teach a number of important social studies concepts. People's motives for moving or migrating can be explored, as can the reasons transportation networks develop in certain places, following certain patterns. Students can also explore the geographic features that make one location preferable to another for human habitation.

DISCUSSION STARTERS

Ask students: Has your family ever moved? Do you know why your family made the move? Did you move from a rural area to a city? The other way around? What did you find exciting about the move? What did you find most difficult? After this discussion, talk about how the western parts of the United States were settled. Discuss the pioneers' motives for going to the West: adventure, the opportunity to own land, the poor economic situation in the East. Have students compare these motives to their own. Also have students project some of the difficulties the pioneers faced. Talk about which are the same as those people who move face today and which are different.

BIBLIOGRAPHY

FOR CHILDREN

Chambers, Catherine. **Log Cabin Home.** Troll, 1984.

Gregory, Kristiana. **Jenny of the Tetons.** Harcourt, 1989.

Sabin, Francene. **Pioneers.** Troll, 1985.

Sabin, Louis. **Paul Bunyan.** Troll, 1985.

Santrey, Laurence. **Oregon Trail.** Troll, 1985.

Turner, Ann. **Dakota Dugout.** Macmillan, 1985.

———. **Grasshopper Summer.** Troll, 1989.

FOR THE TEACHER

Stratton, Joanna. **Pioneer Women: Voices from the Kansas Frontier.** Simon & Schuster, 1981.

West, Elliott. **Growing Up with the Country: Childhood on the Far Western Frontier.** University of New Mexico Press, 1989.

A Letter Home from the Oregon Trail

Begin by presenting to students some background information on the Oregon Trail. Show them a map of the trail, from Independence, Missouri, to Fort Vancouver, in present-day Washington. Try to show the trail against a relief map, to give some idea of the mountainous terrain that the pioneers crossed. You may want to read to students from a book such as Laurence Santrey's *Oregon Trail* (Troll, 1985).

Then have students pretend they are traveling the Oregon Trail with their families. Have them write a letter to a friend back home about their adventures and hardships.

You may want to review the format of a friendly letter with students before they begin. Go over the positioning of the sender's address, date, salutation, and closing. Students might also be interested to know that young people in pioneer times used salutations and closings that were more formal than those they use today. Some examples include: *My dearest* _____; *As ever, Your loving brother*.

Planning for the Long Journey

Remind students that the pioneers were venturing out into a territory with few settlements where they could buy or obtain necessities. Ask students to think carefully about what they would need to take with them if they were pioneers. Remind them that they would need certain items once they reached their destination as well as supplies for the trip. To offer a framework for their thinking, suggest that they use a chart such as the following:

ACTIVITY	ITEMS NEEDED
farming	hoe, plow, seeds
cooking	pots and pans, bowls, spoons, knives

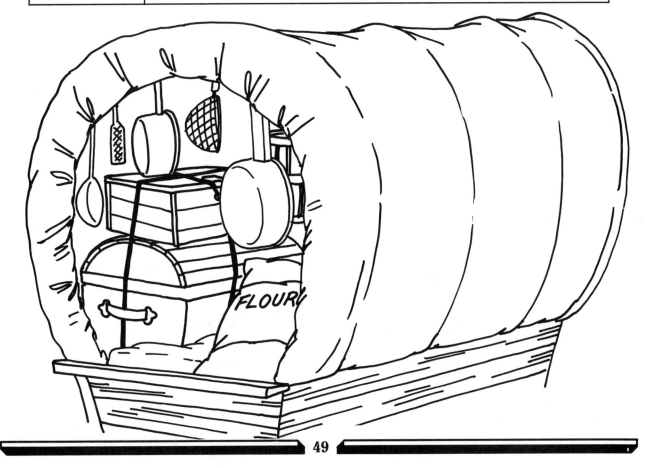

Cowboy Lingo

Tell students that cowboys used many unusual, colorful words and expressions. Many of these came from Spanish, as Spanish-speaking settlers had lived in the Southwest before the cowboys came. Have students work together to make a bulletin board display illustrating a selection of cowboy terms such as *bonanza, brand, bronco, buckaroo, chaparral, chaps, chuck, dogie, dude, lasso, mustang, pemmican, pinto, roundup, rustler, Stetson, spurs, vigilante, wrangler.*

Have students use a square space, as large as your bulletin board or exhibition space permits, to depict and describe each term. Suggest that students use a combination of illustration and written description. In addition to dictionaries and encyclopedias, you may want to have on hand books about cowboys. If a word has a Spanish root, have students give the root word and its meaning. Use a marker and a wide strip of construction paper to title the display "Cowboy Lingo."

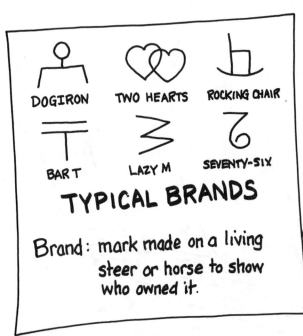

DOGIRON   TWO HEARTS   ROCKING CHAIR

BAR T   LAZY M   SEVENTY-SIX

TYPICAL BRANDS

Brand: mark made on a living steer or horse to show who owned it.

STETSON

Stetson: the cowboy's hat, first made by John Stetson in Philadelphia.

The Further Adventures of Paul Bunyan

Read aloud several tall tales from the Old West. Choose tales about Paul Bunyan, John Henry, Pecos Bill, and other mythical heroes of this era. (Troll publishes a series of tales of our country's great folk heroes—The American Folk Heroes Library. Volumes feature tales of John Henry, Paul Bunyan, Mike Fink, and Pecos Bill, retold for an audience of middle- to upper-elementary students.)

Help students to identify the characteristics of a tall tale. Be sure they understand that exaggeration, adventure, and humor are important elements. You might want to brainstorm with students and list on the chalkboard all the examples of exaggeration that they can find in the tall tales you read to them. Lead a discussion on why certain physical or character traits are exaggerated in these tales.

Have students make up tall tales of their own. Suggest that they make up more zany adventures for Paul Bunyan or another favorite tall-tale character. Perhaps they will want to work with a title such as ''Paul Bunyan Visits the Twenty-First Century.'' Remind students to include exaggeration and humor in their tales.

People Come and Go

The following statistics represent the combined total number of people who came to each region from somewhere else minus the number who left that region in the same period. Explain to students that a negative number means that more people moved out of the region than moved into it.

Internal Migration, 1870–1880

New England (Connecticut, Maine, Massachusetts, New Hampshire, Rhode Island, Vermont) — **141,100**
Middle Atlantic (New Jersey, New York, Pennsylvania) —————————————— **129,200**
East North Central (Illinois, Indiana, Michigan, Ohio, Wisconsin) ——————— **28,300**
West North Central (Iowa, Kansas, Minnesota, Missouri, Nebraska, North Dakota, South Dakota)
——— **868,900**
South Atlantic (Delaware, District of Columbia, Florida, Georgia, Maryland, North Carolina,
   South Carolina, Virginia, West Virginia) —————————————————————— **40,900**
East South Central (Alabama, Kentucky, Mississippi, Tennessee) ——————— **−205,300**
West South Central (Arkansas, Louisiana, Oklahoma, Texas) ——————————— **308,500**
Mountain (Arizona, Colorado, Idaho, Montana, Nevada, New Mexico, Utah, Wyoming) ——— **189,900**
Pacific (Alaska, California, Hawaii, Oregon, Washington) ——————————————— **197,300**

Source: *Historical Statistics of the United States from Colonial Times to 1970.* U.S. Department of Commerce, Bureau of the Census, 1975.

Have students construct a bar graph using these figures. Help them to make a vertical axis that covers the necessary range, and to mark it off properly. Then help them to make the bars the correct height.

Once students have completed their graphs, help them to use the graphs to answer the following questions:

> **1.** Which region lost people from 1870–1880?
>
> **2.** Which region gained the most people?
>
> **3.** Which region gained the next greatest number of people?

Ask students to write a brief paragraph that summarizes the information they were able to infer using the numbers on the chart. For interested students, suggest that they research the factors that played a part in the migration.

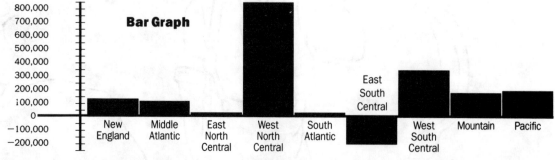

Writing a Report

Have students use the encyclopedia or other sourcebooks to research and write a report on a topic related to United States westward expansion.

First, have each student select a topic of personal interest. Possible topics include the following:

- The Pony Express
- The effect of westward expansion on Native Americans
- Wagon trains
- Cattle trails
- Sod houses

- The contributions of Chinese workers in the building of the transcontinental railroad
- Homesteaders
- The Mexican cowboys

Suggest to students that they begin their reports with a brief statement telling why their topic might be important or interesting to someone studying the Old West. Encourage students to illustrate their reports with drawings, photographs, and other visual aids. When they finish writing, have volunteers share their reports with the rest of the class.

Answers to "Railroads Across America," page 54: **1.** Kansas Pacific; Atchison, Topeka, and Santa Fe **2.** Atchison, Topeka, and Santa Fe **3.** Union Pacific **4.** Kansas Pacific; Atchison, Topeka, and Santa Fe **5.** San Francisco, Los Angeles **6.** Central Pacific and Southern Pacific
Answers to "When and Where in the Wild West," page 55: **1.** 1889, Oklahoma **2.** 1860, Missouri to California **3.** 1873, Illinois **4.** 1869, Utah **5.** 1890, South Dakota **6.** 1849, California **7.** 1862, Washington, D.C. **8.** 1836, Oregon

Railroads Across America

Use the railroad map to answer the questions.

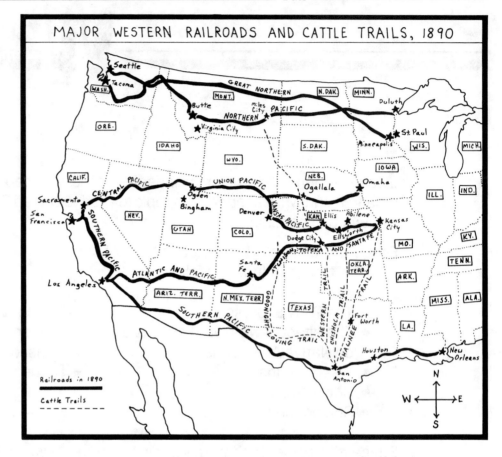

MAJOR WESTERN RAILROADS AND CATTLE TRAILS, 1890

Railroads in 1890 ——————
Cattle Trails - - - - - -

1. Which two railroads intersected the Chisholm Trail? _____

_____

2. As the Atlantic and Pacific Railroad headed east, which railroad did it connect with?

_____

3. Which railroad did the Central Pacific Railroad connect with heading east? _____

_____

4. Which two railroads passed through the state of Kansas? _____

_____

5. What were some large cities on the Southern Pacific Railroad? _____

_____

6. Which two railroads went to San Francisco? _____

_____

When and Where in the Wild West

Draw a line from each event to the correct date and to the correct place. Use the encyclopedia to help you.

Event	**Date**	**Place**
1. Last large land rush	1849	South Dakota
2. The first run is made on the Pony Express	1890	Washington, D.C.
3. Barbed wire invented	1862	California
4. Transcontinental railroad completed	1874	Missouri to California
5. Many Sioux people are killed in battle at Wounded Knee	1836	Oklahoma
6. First large gold rush in the West begins	1889	Utah
7. Homestead act passed	1860	Illinois
8. Missionaries such as Marcus and Narcissa Whitman travel a new trail and settle in the Northwest	1869	Oregon

Reviewing Westward Expansion

Natural Resources

Have students compare and contrast the ways the pioneers used the resources of the West with the ways Native Americans did. You may want to use a chart such as the one below to help students make comparisons. Students can base their answers on information they have gained in the course of their studying units on Native Americans and westward expansion in this book, or on their own research.

	similarities in ways pioneers and Native Americans used them	differences in the ways pioneers and Native Americans used them
buffalo		
gold		
earth		
furs		

Suggest that students draw conclusions from the comparisons and contrasts they have found and discuss them with their classmates.

Frontier Reportage

As a final review activity, ask students to imagine that they are working for a weekly newspaper in a frontier community. Have students select a topic or incident from their reading about westward expansion and plan and write a brief newspaper article about it. Then collect these articles and bind them together into a simulated newspaper.

The Civil War

The Civil War was one of this country's most tragic conflicts. Tensions between North and South had been escalating for more than a decade. The southern economy was dependent on cotton produced largely by slaves. In the North, where the Industrial Revolution was in full swing, people increasingly viewed slavery as unjust. Still, few could have foreseen that the resolution of their conflicts and differences would entail such violence and devastation. Union and Confederate soldiers clashed in scores of battles that did not end for over five years. Over 500,000 Americans lost their lives—more than in any other war in which this nation has fought. The South was reduced to grinding poverty. A deep bitterness lingered between the two sides as northerners set out to "reconstruct" the South after the war's end.

Yet the Civil War also established once and for all the indivisibility of the Union of the United States, led to the abolition of slavery, and strengthened the nation's commitment to treating all U.S. citizens as equals. Students can begin to appreciate the deep and lasting impact of the Civil War by reading historical fiction, studying biographies or firsthand narratives of actual people of the time, or even learning songs of the period.

BIBLIOGRAPHY

FOR CHILDREN

Bains, Rae. **Clara Barton: Angel of the Battlefield.** Troll, 1982.

———— **Robert E. Lee: Brave Leader.** Troll, 1986.

Beatty, Patricia. **Charley Skedaddle.** Troll, 1987.

Chang, Ina. **A Separate Battle: Women and the Civil War.** Dutton, 1991.

Meltzer, Milton. **Voices from the Civil War.** Crowell, 1989.

FOR THE TEACHER

Burns, Ken, producer. **The Civil War.** A documentary television series originally broadcast on PBS in 1990. (VHS videos and audio soundtrack of the series are available.)

Smith, Page. **Trial By Fire: A People's History of the Civil War and Reconstruction.** Penguin, 1990.

Ward, Geoffrey C., with Ric Burns and Ken Burns. **The Civil War: An Illustrated History.** Knopf, 1990.

DISCUSSION STARTERS

Begin discussing the Civil War by reviewing background—the debate over slavery and the quarrel over states' rights—and the war's basic chronology. You can then go on to explore the many aspects of this period in greater depth, using the activities that follow this page at appropriate points in your lessons.

Read aloud the chapter "The Battle of the Wilderness" from *Charley Skedaddle* (Troll, 1987), a book about a young boy who deserts the Union Army. Ask students what they would have done if they had been in Charley's place (1) when he saw his friend Jem go down, and (2) after he had killed his first "Johnny Reb."

The Economic War

The condition of a country's economy largely determines its ability to fight a war effectively. In turn, a war has a tremendous effect on a nation's economy. In studying the Civil War, it is important for students to understand that the North was much better economically prepared for war than the South, primarily because of the Industrial Revolution, which was mainly a northern phenomenon. Students should also be helped to see that the Civil War had the effect of bringing the South into the Industrial Age.

Ask students: What goods are used when a nation fights a war? What raw materials and facilities are needed to provide these goods? Have the class brainstorm answers to these questions and record them on the chalkboard. Help students to be thorough in their thinking by asking questions such as: How could soldiers quickly travel across land or water? What is needed on the battlefield? How are soldiers and civilians to be clothed and fed?

Then present the class with the following statistics:

Total Population: the North had 2.5 times more people than the South
Miles of Railroad: the North had 2.4 times more than the South
Naval Ships: the North had 25 times the tonnage of ships as the South
Factory Production: the North produced 10 times more than the South
Textile Goods Production: the North produced 14 times more than the South
Iron Production: 15 times greater in the North than in the South
Coal Production: 38 times greater in the North than in the South
Firearms Production: 32 times greater in the North than in the South
Acres of Farmland: 3 times more in the North than in the South
Cotton Production: 24 times greater in the South than in the North

---

(Source: Norton, Mary Beth. *A People and a Nation: A History of the United States*, vol. 1 [Houghton Mifflin, 1982].)

Using these statistics, ask students to draw conclusions about the different degrees of readiness for war between the North and the South. Have students do library research to find out how the Confederacy tried to cope with its economic and technological disadvantages. Then invite students to write monologues from the point of view of either a southern civilian or a soldier in the Confederate army. In their monologues, students can describe the things they need but do not have because of the South's economic crisis, and how they make the most of what they have.

Songs of the Civil War

Explain to students that soldiers in the Civil War had much free time on their hands. Battles occurred infrequently, and few lasted more than a few days. One of the most popular diversions for both Yankee and Confederate troops was singing. Every battle inspired new songs. Black regiments introduced their tradition of spirituals and ''freedom'' songs. Each side had a battery of songs all its own, yet some songs were sung by both the Blue and the Gray.

Use a book such as *I Hear America Singing!* by Hazel Arnett (Praeger, 1975) to introduce students to several of the well-known songs of this era. Many of them are very moving and capture the deep feelings the war aroused in Americans. ''Dixie'' was a song of fondness for home in the South, ''Battle Hymn of the Republic'' was a patriotic song that inspired courage in the North, and songs such as ''Tenting Tonight on the Old Camp Ground'' made light of military life on both sides of the Mason-Dixon line.

Have students form small groups and have each group choose and learn one song from this era to perform for the rest of the class.

Tenting Tonight

We're tenting tonight on the old campground;
Give us a song to cheer
Our weary hearts, a song of home
And friends we love so dear.
Many are the hearts that are weary tonight, wishing for war to cease;
Many are the hearts looking for the right to see the dream of peace.
Tenting tonight, tenting tonight, tenting on the old campground.

A Field Trip to the Red Cross

Explain to students that the woman who played a central role in the founding of the American Red Cross, Clara Barton, was motivated by her experience nursing the wounded in Civil War battles. After learning about the good works of this new organization in Europe, Clara Barton led the campaign for an American chapter and was appointed its first president. Explain to students the terrible conditions wounded soldiers faced at the time of the Civil War, when medical care was scarce and crude, and anesthesia was nonexistent. The American branch of the Red Cross was founded in 1881 by Barton and others in part because they were horrified by the suffering these men endured.

Tell students that since its early days, the Red Cross has grown and expanded its aims. Today it seeks to relieve many different kinds of misery, both in time of war and in time of peace. In addition to providing medical care and supplies, the Red Cross helps families to communicate with their relatives in the armed forces while they are off at war and teaches first aid and child care.

Have the class take a field trip to your local Red Cross chapter, so that students can find out firsthand the many different services this organization offers.

Prior to the trip, have students form small groups. Have each group choose a different area to investigate during the trip. You might have students choose from the following areas:

    services to members of the armed forces
    services to disaster victims
    blood program
    safety and health programs
    youth programs

Clara Barton
1821–1912

Groups might be encouraged to research and report on the history of the Red Cross at the local, national, or international level. After the trip, have each group organize its findings to write a report. Then have a group member present the report to the class. The class may want to combine the information they compile into a booklet, a sort of guide to their community's Red Cross.

Famous Generals of the Civil War

The Civil War produced many famous generals. Both the Union and the Confederacy had commanders who were admired for their bravery, military genius, and colorful personalities. Becoming more familiar with these figures can help to bring the historical era to life for students.

Have each student choose one general from the following list (each general can be chosen by more than one student) and have him or her write a thumbnail sketch, featuring the highlights of his military career.

UNION	CONFEDERACY
Ulysses S. Grant	Pierre Beauregard
George McClellan	Stonewall Jackson
George Meade	Robert E. Lee
William Sherman	George Pickett
George Thomas	Jeb Stuart

Use this exercise to help students practice summarizing information and to help them distinguish more important from less important information. Provide students with a form on which to write their sketches. You may want to use an enlarged version of the form shown below. Emphasize to students that in choosing what to include in their sketches, they should focus on the key facts about their subject's life and only the most noteworthy highlights of his career.

SKETCH OF: _____
BORN: _____
_____ DIED: _____

What Would You Have Done?

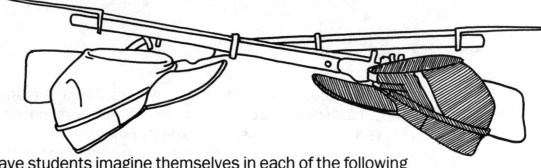

Have students imagine themselves in each of the following situations. Ask them to describe how they would have felt and acted and why. Have students compare their responses.

1. You are a Confederate soldier in the Battle of Gettysburg. You have just been given the command to charge. You know that Union troops surround you on all sides. You know the odds of your surviving are slim.

2. You are a northerner whose family is well-to-do. You have just been drafted, but you can afford to pay for a replacement to serve in your place. You support the Union cause, but you also are aware that Union troops have been suffering heavy losses.

3. You are a southern soldier who has been fighting for the Confederacy for over two years. You receive a letter from your wife in which she tells you that she and your two children are nearly starving back home. You contemplate deserting to return home and manage the family farm.

4. You are a northern black man who is proud to serve in the Union army. You have discovered that white soldiers of the same rank are receiving higher pay and an allowance for their uniforms (whereas you had to pay for yours out of your own pocket).

5. You are a southern woman whose husband has just gone off to fight. You have several children and are used to devoting your time chiefly to their care and to household duties. You have almost no knowledge of how to manage the farm.

   Students may want to use one of the above situations as the basis for a historical short story.

Equality in the Armed Forces

Discuss with students the changing role of black soldiers in the Civil War. At first they were not allowed to serve at all; then they were allowed to enlist but were assigned to special regiments that did menial work but saw no active combat; finally, toward the end of the war, they were allowed to serve in combat duty. Integrated regiments were never introduced.

Today we take it for granted that soldiers of all backgrounds will serve their country, side by side, in all forms of military endeavor. Ask students to think about whether this is true of women soldiers in the armed forces.

Divide the class into an even number of small groups. Tell half the groups to prepare to debate arguments in favor of the following proposition, the other half to prepare arguments against it:

> **Resolved:** that women and men in the U.S. armed forces should be subject to the same regulations, and that they should share equally in all duties.

Use a modified version of standard debate format: begin with each side presenting its arguments, followed by opportunity for rebuttal. (You may want to set time limits for each student's presentation.)

Answers to "Reading a Battle Map," page 65: **1.** an arrow **2.** a row of squares **3.** about 36 miles (22 km) **4.** they found a defense set up by General Lee **5.** it was where many railroad lines intersected

 # The Gettysburg Address

Four score and seven years ago our fathers brought forth on this continent, a new nation, conceived in Liberty, and dedicated to the proposition that all men are created equal.

Now we are engaged in a great civil war, testing whether that nation, or any nation so conceived and so dedicated, can long endure. We are met on a great battlefield of that war. We have come to dedicate a portion of that field, as a final resting place for those who here gave their lives that that nation might live. It is altogether fitting and proper that we should do this.

But, in a larger sense, we can not dedicate—we can not consecrate—we can not hallow—this ground. The brave men, living and dead, who struggled here, have consecrated it, far above our poor power to add or detract. The world will little note, nor long remember what we say here, but it can never forget what they did here. It is for us the living, rather, to be dedicated here to the unfinished work which they who fought here have thus far so nobly advanced. It is rather for us to be here dedicated to the great task remaining before us—that from these honored dead we take increased devotion to that cause for which they gave the last full measure of devotion—that we here highly resolve that these dead shall not have died in vain—that this nation, under God, shall have a new birth of freedom—and that government of the people, by the people, for the people, shall not perish from the earth.

Work with a partner to create a paraphrase—that is, a retelling in your own words—of Lincoln's Gettysburg Address.

_____

_____

_____

_____

_____

_____

_____

_____

_____

_____

_____

Practice your speech, then deliver it to the class.

Reading a Battle Map

Use the map of General Grant's siege of Petersburg, Virginia, to answer the questions below.

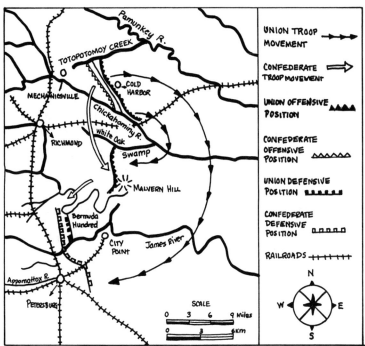

1. What kind of symbol is used to show troops that were moving?

_____

2. What kind of symbol is used to show troops that remained stationary, in defensive positions?

_____

3. About how many miles (kilometers) did General Grant's troops march from Cold Harbor to Petersburg?

_____

4. What did General Grant's men find when they reached Petersburg?

_____

5. Based on the information on the map, why do you think Petersburg was an important city for either side to hold?

_____

Reviewing the Civil War

Civil War Time Line

Have the class make a time line of the major events of the Civil War. Divide the class into four groups, one for each year of the war. Have the groups use history textbooks or the encyclopedia to identify and learn about the principal events of their designated years. Have them display their findings on large pieces of construction paper or butcher paper, with the time line running horizontally. Encourage students to select the one or two most important events of their year and to illustrate them on the appropriate sections of the time line.

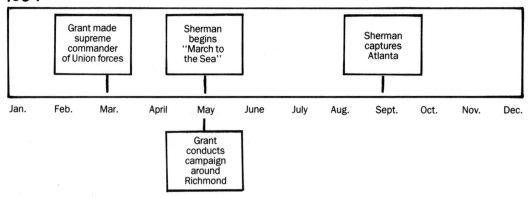

Life in an Army Camp

Have students imagine that they are soldiers in either the Union army or the Confederate army camped along the Rappahannock River in Virginia during the late fall of 1862, before the battle of Fredericksburg. (At that time divisions from both armies camped on opposite sides of the river, so close to each other that they could hear each other singing.) Encourage them to read about that moment in history, in history textbooks or the encyclopedia. Have them write a diary entry in which they describe their life in camp and reflect on the conflict in which they are involved.

Immigration

It has been estimated that nearly half of all Americans today are the descendants of the twelve to sixteen million immigrants who came to this country around the turn of the century. Many more are immigrants who have come to the United States in recent decades. Teachers can use firsthand accounts, biographies, role-playing, and fiction to help bring the immigrant experience to life.

Immigrants have come for many reasons, but nearly all hoped to find a life of prosperity and freedom in America. Most had to cope with numerous hardships as they strove to make their dreams a reality: difficult ocean voyages; sweatshop conditions in factories; discrimination; and tensions between parents who held onto the language and customs of the old country and their children, who had been assimilated into mainstream American life. In spite of such hardships, immigrants from all over the world have not only become successful in the United States, but have also enriched the nation culturally, intellectually, and economically.

BIBLIOGRAPHY

FOR CHILDREN

Bunting, Eve. **How Many Days to America?** Clarion, 1988.

Jacobs, William Jay. **Ellis Island: New Hope in a New Land.** Scribner's, 1990.

Koller, Jackie French. **Nothing to Fear.** Harcourt Brace Jovanovich, 1991.

Reimers, David. **The Immigrant Experience.** Chelsea House, 1988.

FOR THE TEACHER

Davis, Marilyn P. **Mexican Voices/American Dreams: An Oral History of Mexican Immigration to the United States.** Holt, 1990.

Morrison, Joan and Charlotte Zabusky. **American Mosaic: The Immigrant Experience in the Words of Those Who Lived It.** Dutton, 1980.

Tenhula, John. **Voices from Southeast Asia: The Refugee Experience in the United States.** Holmes & Meier, 1991.

DISCUSSION STARTERS

Ask students to interview a relative or neighbor who emigrated to this country. In their interviews, have them inquire about the reasons people had for leaving their old country and coming to the United States, the problems they encountered when they arrived, the rewards they have found in their new lives here. Have students share their responses with the class. Discuss the similarities and differences in what they found.

America's Immigrants

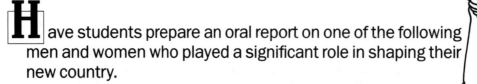

Have students prepare an oral report on one of the following men and women who played a significant role in shaping their new country.

Leo H. Baekeland
(chemist, from Belgium)

Alexander Graham Bell
(inventor, from Scotland)

Irving Berlin
(songwriter, from Russia)

Frank Capra
(motion picture director, from Sicily)

Willem de Kooning
(painter, from the Netherlands)

Albert Einstein
(physicist, from Germany)

Ernesto Galarza
(historian/civil rights leader, from Mexico)

Greta Garbo
(actress, from Sweden)

Walter Gropius
(architect, from Germany)

Meyer Guggenheim
(industrialist, from Switzerland)

Mary H. Jones
(labor leader, from Ireland)

Joseph Pulitzer
(journalist, from Hungary)

Ben Shahn
(painter, from Lithuania)

Isaac Bashevis Singer
(writer, from Poland)

Igor Stravinsky
(composer, from Russia)

Chien-shiung Wu
(physicist, from China)

While students are preparing their reports, suggest that they focus not just on their subject's achievements, but also on how the person adjusted to life in the United States. Did he or she encounter any barriers or difficulties? What was it about this country that he or she came to appreciate most? Was the person able to retain his or her cultural heritage in the new milieu?

You might suggest that students use the following structure when organizing their information:

1. Life in the old country; reasons for coming to the U.S.
2. Initial adjustment to life in the U.S.
3. Growing up personally and professionally in the U.S.
4. Major contributions and accomplishments
5. The person's reflections on the new country
6. The person's insights into the role of his or her cultural heritage

Becoming a United States Citizen

Invite a naturalized citizen to speak to the class about how he or she became a United States citizen. Suggest that your guest speaker cover the following areas when speaking to the class:

- reasons for seeking U.S. citizenship
- the various steps in the process
- what U.S. citizenship means to the person today

You might also ask him or her to describe in detail the swearing-in ceremony and tell (if he or she wishes) about the feelings he or she had while participating in the ceremony.

Ask students to listen carefully for the steps in the naturalization process. Have them take notes. You might want to follow up the speaker's visit with a class discussion of what citizenship means to new immigrants and discuss with students the following requirements for naturalization:

- live in the U.S for at least five years prior to seeking naturalization
- show a basic understanding of the U.S. political system
- demonstrate elementary knowledge of the English language
- prove that he or she has lived an upright life and has not in the last ten years supported any political belief or system antagonistic to the U.S.
- swear an oath of loyalty to the U.S.

Looking at the Immigration Policies

Begin by brainstorming with students a variety of reasons people might immigrate to the United States from different parts of the world. Then introduce students to the issues involved in setting immigration policies:

- Does the U.S. government have an obligation to provide a home and human services (which cost taxpayers' money) to all who seek to live here? Or at least to all refugees?
- Will immigrants take jobs that otherwise might go to Americans?
- If quotas are necessary, and some immigrants are allowed to come while others are not, what should be the basis for such quotas?

Familiarize students with current immigration policies as set forth in the Immigration Act of 1965, the Refugee Act of 1980, and the Immigration Reform and Control Act of 1986.

The Immigration Act of 1965 permitted people to come to the United States on a first-come, first-serve basis. National quotas were abolished and replaced by hemispheric ones. In 1978 they were revised to a single annual global quota. Immigrants with close relatives who are American citizens, those with skills needed in the United States, and political refugees were given preference. Under old immigration laws, fewer than 200,000 people were permitted to enter the United States each year. From 1965 on, 290,000 people were allowed to enter. **The Refugee Act of 1980** allowed an additional 50,000 political refugees to be admitted annually to the country. **The Immigration Reform and Control Act of 1986** outlawed the employment of illegal aliens but gave amnesty to all illegal aliens who had entered the United States before 1982.

Have students write essays explaining why they think a certain aspect of current U.S. immigration policy either is or is not fair. Have them give concrete reasons for their opinions. If they do not think it is fair, have them propose modifications to the existing policy that will make it fair for all immigrants.

Immigration Trends in a Line Graph

Remind students that graphs help people visualize certain types of information. In this activity and the following one (page 72), students will construct different types of graphs to present different types of information about immigration trends in the United States.

Have students study the following chart and use the figures to construct a line graph showing how the number of legal immigrants to the U.S. has risen and fallen over the years.

Year	Number of Immigrants	Year	Number of Immigrants
1820	8,400	1910	1,041,600
1830	23,300	1920	430,000
1840	84,100	1930	242,000
1850	370,000	1940	70,800
1860	153,600	1950	249,200
1870	387,200	1960	265,400
1880	457,300	1970	373,300
1890	455,300	1980	530,600
1900	448,600	1988	643,000

Source: U.S. Department of Immigration and Naturalization

Suggest that students divide up their vertical axis into increments of 200,000.

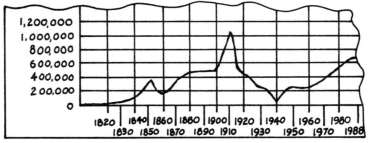

You may wish to discuss with students the reasons for the sudden decreases and increases in immigration, such as the enactment of new legislations and the changes in the world's geopolitical situation.

Immigration Trends in a Pie Graph

Explain to students that while a line graph helps us to visualize changes over time, a pie graph helps us to view something in relation to the whole at any given moment.

Have students construct a pie graph showing the various nations from which the most people immigrated to the United States in 1988. Have students study the following chart.

Number of Legal Immigrants to the U.S. in 1988

Mexico	95,500	Dominican Republic	27,200
Philippines	50,700	India	26,300
Haiti	34,800	Vietnam	25,800
South Korea	34,700	Jamaica	21,000
China	28,700	Cuba	17,600
Other Countries	280,700		

Source: U.S. Department of Immigration and Naturalization

Provide help in constructing the pie graph, as necessary. (First students will need to convert each of the above figures into a percentage of the total number of immigrants [643,000] by dividing it by 643,000 and multiplying the answer by 100. If they wish, students can use a calculator.)

Next, provide students with needed help in visualizing how big a "slice of the pie" each of these percentages will represent. It may help students to remember that one quarter of the pie is 25 percent, and a "five-minute" segment on the pie is about 8 percent. Be sure to tell students that the whole pie represents the total number of legal immigrants who entered the United States in 1988.

Interested students may wish to research and follow the fluctuations of individual immigrant groups over four or five consecutive years. Encourage students to find and explain the factors that affect these changes.

The Immigration Process

Review with students the various steps immigrants had to go through as they were "processed" at Ellis Island during the years 1891–1915.

1. Store baggage (pay a company that provided this service)

2. Undergo medical examination
    a. Some were detained in designated areas for further examination
    b. Some were quarantined and treated
    c. Some were sent to the "mental room"

3. Undergo the primary, or legal, inspection
    a. Every immigrant was asked a long series of personal questions (Explain to students that owing to fear of being rejected and language barriers—despite the use of interpreters—many immigrants were very flustered by this experience.)
    b. About 20 percent of immigrants were held for further questioning by a board, to determine whether these people were likely to become public charges (Explain to students that a public charge is someone who depends on the government for basic needs.)

4. Proceed to social services area
    a. Enlist help of immigrant aid societies to find relatives
    b. Send telegrams

5. Change money to American currency

6. Proceed to railroad ticket office to purchase ticket (Many immigrants were swindled out of their money at this stage. Dishonest people would sell the immigrants counterfeit tickets, which the railroad would then refuse to honor.)
    OR
    Proceed to New York Room, to await government ferry for New York City

After reviewing these steps with students, have them show the process graphically using a flow chart. After students have made their flow charts, you may wish to have them role-play several immigrants and the various officials they meet during the immigration process.

Answers to "Words From Other Lands," page 75: **1.** d **2.** b **3.** a **4.** j **5.** c **6.** g **7.** d **8.** e **9.** i **10.** b **11.** g **12.** f **13.** j **14.** h **15.** a **16.** i **17.** c **18.** h **19.** f **20.** e

Working on Ellis Island

Suppose you are a worker on Ellis Island in 1915. You might be an inspector, an interpreter, a doctor, a cook, a money changer, or some other type of worker. Complete the sentences below.

1. I work as a _____ on Ellis Island.

2. These are some of the people and things I see every day at work: _____

_____

_____

_____

_____

_____

_____

3. These are some of the responsibilities I have at work: _____

_____

_____

_____

_____

_____

_____

On a separate sheet of paper, describe a memorable incident from work: a time when you met a very interesting person, or a time when something unusual or special happened.

Words from Other Lands

American English is full of words from the languages spoken by immigrants. Match each word with its language of origin. Use a dictionary with etymologies (word histories). You will use each language twice.

1. delicatessen _____
2. patio _____
3. schmaltz _____
4. ghetto _____
5. polka _____
6. cookie _____
7. kindergarten _____
8. chowder _____
9. smorgasbord _____
10. ranch _____
11. boss _____
12. tycoon _____
13. pizza _____
14. judo _____
15. phooey _____
16. ski _____
17. robot _____
18. kamikaze _____
19. chop suey _____
20. prairie _____

a. Yiddish

b. Spanish

c. Slavic languages

d. German

e. French

f. Chinese

g. Dutch

h. Japanese

i. Scandinavian languages

j. Italian

Reviewing Immigration

Letter to the Old Country

Have students pretend they are recent immigrants to the United States. Have them write a letter to a family member or friend whom they have left behind in the old country. Encourage any student whose family emigrated from a particular country fairly recently (within one or two generations) to use that as his or her country of origin. Urge these students to speak to grandparents or other older relatives about what their life was like in the old country and what was most memorable about their transition to life in the United States.

Students will probably want to include remarks on the following subjects in their letters:

- What the trip to their new home was like
- How customs are different from those in the old country
- Any problems they are having; people or items they miss most
- Whatever might convince the friend or relative to come and join them in the United States

A United Nation

The motto of the United States is *e pluribus unum* (out of many, one). As a class, discuss the significance of these words. Have students consider the problems that could be encountered in trying to forge a single and united nation of people from many different backgrounds. Students could respond by saying that people might remain more loyal to the customs and concerns of their own ethnic group than to the nation as a whole, or lose touch with their roots in the process of Americanization. After the class discussion, have students write a composition laying out a solution to these problems and setting forth a way for the United States to live up to its motto.

In 1850, less than 20 percent of Americans lived in cities. By 1900, nearly 40 percent of the country's population were urban residents. During this same period, between 1850 and 1900, the size of many American cities also grew enormously. The population of Chicago more than tripled between 1880 and 1900. As cities grew, they changed. Many features of today's cities had their origins at this time. New modes of transportation, such as the streetcar, were developed; a new kind of store, the department store, was born; the invention of the elevator and innovations in the field of engineering allowed tall buildings called skyscrapers to be built; and a host of new forms of entertainment and recreation, from professional baseball to vaudeville, became popular. Many contemporary urban problems, from slums to corruption in government, also first became acute at this time.

Today, the majority of Americans are city dwellers. It is important for students to understand the complex nature of urban life and how its institutions and attractions—as well as problems—originated and developed. Field trips and interviews can be especially helpful in the study of city life. Students can also develop an appreciation for the enormous amount of thought and planning that lies behind a functioning city by trying their own hand at planning a small project, such as a city building or park.

DISCUSSION STARTERS

Ask students the following questions about city life:
- What cities have you lived in or visited?
- What was the largest city you have ever visited?
- As a visitor, what did you like about the city? What did you not like?
- If you could live in any city in the world, which would it be?
- What would you like about living in a city? What would you not like?
- If you owned a prosperous company in the suburbs looking to relocate in a city, what would attract you to the city? What would deter you?

BIBLIOGRAPHY

FOR CHILDREN
Bunting, Eve. **The Hideout.** Harcourt, 1991.

Fox, Paula. **Monkey Island.** Orchard, 1991.

Greenberg, Jan. **Just the Two of Us.** Farrar, Straus & Giroux, 1988.

Macaulay, David. **City: A Story of Roman Planning and Construction.** Houghton Mifflin, 1983.

Santrey, Laurence. **State and Local Government.** Troll, 1985.

Von Tscharner, Renata and Fleming, Ronald L. **New Providence: A Changing Cityscape.** Harcourt, 1987.

FOR THE TEACHER
Chudacoff, H. and J. Smith. **The Evolution of American Urban Society.** Third edition. Prentice Hall, 1988.

Mumford, Lewis. **The City in History.** Harcourt, 1968.

Cities and Technology

In order to help students realize the degree to which modern cities are dependent on technology, have the class brainstorm everything that normally happens in a city that would be impossible without electricity. Suggest that they consider the activities or events that happen in different city places: residential buildings, office buildings, stores, restaurants, theaters, subways, streets, and so on.

You might want to divide the class in half, have each half brainstorm on its own, then have them come back together to consolidate both lists.

Be sure students consider the effects of the absence of some of the following:

traffic lights

doorbells

elevators

neon signs

subways

word processors

computers

fax machines

telephones

Cities in Song

Sing the chorus of "Meet Me in St. Louis, Louis." Have any students who know it join in.

"Meet me in St. Lou - is, Lou - is, Meet me at the fair, _____ Don't tell me the lights are shin - ing a - ny place but there; _____ We will dance the Hooch - ee Kooch - ee, _____ I will be your toots - ie woots - ie; If you will meet me in St. Lou - is, Lou - is, Meet me at the fair." _____

Invite students to write new lyrics to the chorus of "Meet Me in St. Louis, Louis," substituting the name of another city. Point out that the original lyrics ("Meet me at the fair . . .Don't tell me the lights are shining any place but there") sing the praises of one of the great events in St. Louis' history —the World's Fair of 1904. Have students think of something associated with the city they are singing about—a sports event or team, a new building, a street festival. Encourage them to share their new versions with the class.

Designing City Buildings

A sk students to think about the following kinds of buildings, all of which can be found in a typical city:

1. A school building
2. An office building with room for ten or more different businesses
3. A department store that sells clothing, furniture, appliances, toys, and most other products customers need
4. A public library with the most up-to-date audio, visual, and computer equipment
5. An entertainment center, made up of a movie theater and any other activities students think might attract people

Have students form five groups, and assign one type of building to each group. Then have groups design an ideal version of the building they have been assigned. Point out to students that they should begin by listing the goals that each building might be designed to achieve and then use those goals in deciding what their building should be like.

Seeing City Services in Operation Firsthand

Plan a class field trip to the headquarters of a city service such as the fire department, police department, parks department, or sanitation department. Have older students go with the intention of gathering information to present a report to younger students. Have them prepare an outline of the topics they will want to cover in their presentation. Some ideas might include the following:

- What specific services this department provides for city residents
- What a typical working day is like for an employee in this department, including hours, duties, and so on
- Interesting information on the volume of work done, amount of equipment owned, number of men and women employed, and so on

Help students to prepare the questions they need to ask employees at these city services departments. Arrange the tour well in advance, and advise department officials that students are seeking certain kinds of information and will ask questions of employees.

If possible, provide an opportunity for students to present their reports to younger classes in your school.

Designing a City Park

Parks were designed to offer residents of cities *much needed* space for quiet and recreation. Since the mid-1800s, city planners have recognized the need for areas where city residents can enjoy grass, trees, flowers, and outdoor leisure activities. As an example, you may want to tell students about Frederick Law Olmsted's farsighted plan for Central Park in New York City.

Have students think carefully about everything a city dweller might want in an ideal park. Encourage them to think ''big''—a playground, a small pond for boating, a skating rink, nature trails, even wildlife.

Then have students make a detailed plan of their imaginary park. It should include the placement of all facilities and an idea of where various kinds of trees, shrubs, and other plants will be planted.

Display the completed plans in the classroom.

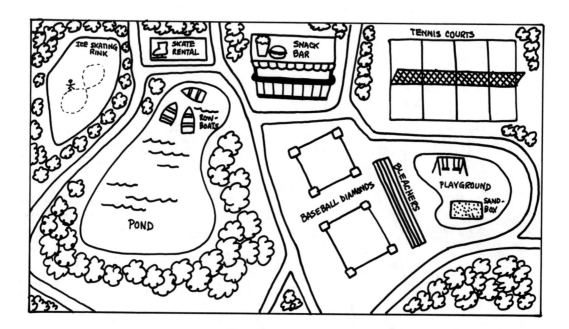

Cities Near Water

American cities grew up where they did for good reasons. Often, those reasons had a lot to do with geographical location. Some cities grew by waterfalls that could provide hydroelectric power. Other cities grew near bodies of water that large ships could reach safely: where one river joined another, at the point where a river ceased being navigable by large ships, at the mouth of a river, or where a protected bay made a good harbor for oceangoing ships. Ships must have access to cities in order to make trade possible. Have students use maps to determine why each of the cities below grew up near certain water sources.

1. Buffalo, New York
   (where the Niagara River joins lakes Erie and Ontario)

2. Pierre, South Dakota
   (on the Missouri River)

3. Duluth, Minnesota
   (good harbor on the end of a lake)

4. Salt Lake City, Utah
   (on the only source of water in the area)

5. Denver, Colorado
   (on a river, at the foot of mountains)

6. San Francisco, California
   (good harbor)

7. Petersburg, Virginia
   (where a river becomes navigable for larger ships)

8. Tampa, Florida
   (good harbor)

9. Philadelphia, Pennsylvania
   (where a river leading to the ocean becomes navigable for large ships)

10. New Orleans, Louisiana
    (at the mouth of the Mississippi River)

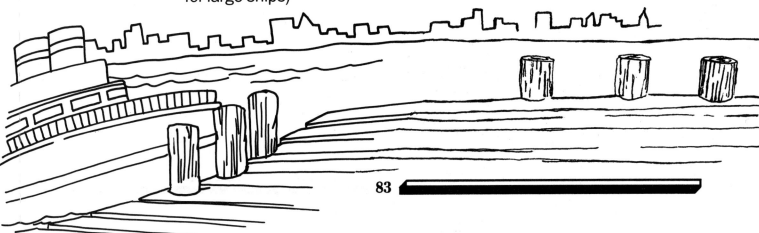

American Cities

Use an almanac to find the following information about each American city listed below:
> population
> area in square miles (square kilometers)
> altitude
> tallest building and its height

1. Atlanta, Georgia
population _____
area _____
altitude _____
tallest building _____

2. Philadelphia, Pennsylvania
population _____
area _____
altitude _____
tallest building _____

3. Boston, Massachusetts
population _____
area _____
altitude _____
tallest building _____

4. Richmond, Virginia
population _____
area _____
altitude _____
tallest building _____

5. Chicago, Illinois
population _____
area _____
altitude _____
tallest building _____

6. St. Louis, Missouri
population _____
area _____
altitude _____
tallest building _____

7. Houston, Texas
population _____
area _____
altitude _____
tallest building _____

8. San Francisco, California
population _____
area _____
altitude _____
tallest building _____

9. New York, New York
population _____
area _____
altitude _____
tallest building _____

10. Seattle, Washington
population _____
area _____
altitude _____
tallest building _____

Which city has the largest population? _____

Which city covers the greatest area? _____

Which city is farthest above sea level? _____

Which city boasts the tallest building? _____

Comparing City, Suburb, and Country

Use the Venn diagram below to compare the ways cities, suburbs, and rural areas are alike and different.

In the parts of the circles labeled "city," "suburb," and "country," list the things that are unique to life in each type of area; that is, things about each one not found in either of the other two.

In area #1, list elements common to country and city life, but not found in suburbs.
In area #2, list elements common to country and suburban life, but not found in cities.
In area #3, list elements common to city and suburban life, but not found in the country.

Finally, in area #4, list elements common to all three areas.

Use another piece of paper if you need more space.

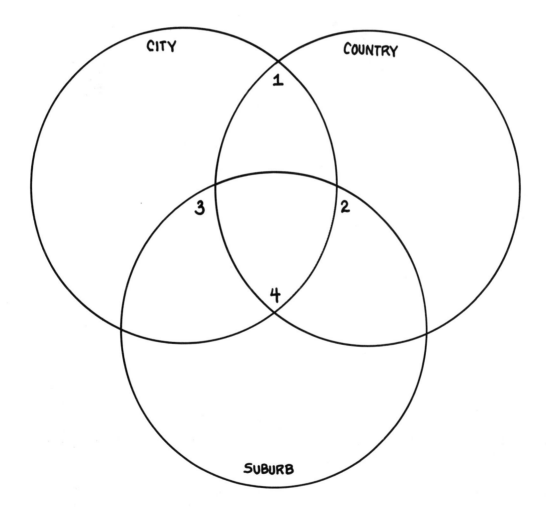

Reviewing City Life

Come to the City!

Have students use the encyclopedia to research various aspects of city life. Possible topics include:

subways	business
traffic control	urban renewal
parks	crime
skyscrapers	political system
waste disposal	playgrounds

Have students work with the information as a class to prepare a public relations brochure designed to attract large companies to return to America's cities. (You might explain that many companies have moved from cities to nearby suburbs. The most common reasons given for such a move are that suburbs tend to have lower crime rates, cleaner streets and public facilities, and more space than city locations can offer.) The brochure might have such subheads as ''Sophisticated Transportation Network,'' ''Exciting New Residential Areas,'' ''Many Services Provided,'' and even ''City Problems—On the Mend.'' Have students divide up the research and the writing. When putting together their final version and assembling an actual brochure, they may want to contact the chamber of commerce of a nearby city for brochures that contain photos they could use.

A frica today is a complex continent, and one that is constantly changing. Most of the nations that make up modern Africa have been self-governing for twenty years or more. In Liberia and other countries, women serve equally with men in government, law, and medicine. Today African nations are world leaders in the production of diamonds, gold, copper, coffee, and many other desirable products. Their governments have successfully promoted cooperation among hundreds of different African peoples who speak nearly 800 different languages. As their economies have become more industrialized, Africans have also found creative solutions to the problem of preserving traditional customs while modernizing in important ways.

Young people are naturally intrigued by Africa's animals, vegetation, and mineral resources (Africa is the world's diamond mining center), and the rich and colorful heritages of its peoples. Upper elementary students will also find it easy to develop an understanding of African nations' struggles for freedom and the right to rule themselves. In addition to strengthening interest in Africa's natural resources, teachers can strive to develop an appreciation in students of the great strides made by Africans in recent years.

DISCUSSION STARTERS

Find out how much students already know about the continent of Africa. Have the class list as many African countries, animals native to Africa, and special natural features of the continent as they can.

Show a recent video or filmstrip about Africa and discuss students' reactions. What did they see or learn about Africa from the viewing that came as a surprise to them? Some good videos put out by National Geographic include *African Odyssey* (1988) and the *Africa* video in their Physical Geography of the Continents series (1991).

Because many nations in Africa have won their independence only recently, Africans value independence very highly. Ask students why they think a nation would place a lot of value on independence. What might be some advantages of being independent?

BIBLIOGRAPHY

FOR CHILDREN
Naidoo, Beverly. **Journey to Jo'burg.** Lippincott, 1986.

Sabin, Francene. **Africa.** Troll, 1985.

Stanley, Diane, and Vennema, Peter. **Shaka, King of the Zulus.** Morrow. 1988.

Steptoe, John. **Mufaro's Beautiful Daughters.** Lothrop, Lee & Shepard, 1987.

Williams, Karen Lynn. **When Africa Was Home.** Orchard, 1991.

FOR THE TEACHER
Bentsen, Cheryl. **Maasai Days.** Summit, 1989.

Lelyveld, Joseph. **Move Your Shadow: South Africa Black and White.** Penguin, 1986.

Naipaul, V.S. **A Bend in the River.** Random, 1989.

Whitaker, Jennifer Seymour. **How Can Africa Survive?** Harper, 1988.

Ancient African Cultures

Divide the class into several groups. Have each group research one of the ancient African civilizations and kingdoms listed below. Then have the class work together to create a chart showing the information they have gathered in a manner that makes it easy to assimilate.

Monomotapa	Kongo
Benin	Ife
Egypt	Mali
Ghana	Songhai
Kush	

Categories students should consider using in their chart include:

dates of rise and fall

food sources

arts

role of trade

reasons for rise and fall

Nelson Mandela: An African Freedom Fighter

Nelson Mandela
(born 1918)

Discuss with students the issue of apartheid, South Africa's strict policy of racial segregation. Point out that in June 1991, the government repealed several major features of the apartheid law, and this action was due in part to the efforts of Nelson Mandela.

Mandela began working to change South Africa's apartheid system in the 1940s. He wanted to do away with this system of government, because under its laws people were treated differently based on their race and black Africans in particular were denied rights and privileges that whites were accorded.

"I have dedicated my life to this struggle of the African people," said Mandela, at the time of his trial at Rivonia in 1964. "I have fought against white domination, and I have fought against black domination. I have cherished the ideal of a democratic and free society in which all persons live together in harmony with equal opportunities."

Perhaps the most dramatic period of his life's struggle for social justice was the seventeen months between March 1961 and August 1962. For eight years before that period, Mandela had been silenced by the government for his efforts to win rights for South Africa's blacks. For more than four of those years he had been on trial for treason. When he was at last found not guilty, Mandela decided to risk his career, his family, and his life in order to renew efforts to fight apartheid and lead new actions for a nonracial constitution for South Africa. For the next seventeen months, Mandela lived in hiding from the police, surfacing only to speak at political gatherings. On August 5, 1962, Nelson Mandela was finally captured. He was imprisoned until February 11, 1990.

Have students work in groups to write short dramatic skits that will bring to life key moments in Nelson Mandela's life. There are several biographies available for young readers. Or you may simply tell the class significant parts of Nelson Mandela's life story, such as his arrests, his trials, his stays in prison, his recent national tour, his successes against apartheid, and his speeches that reflect his antiapartheid philosophies.

Droughts in Africa

Drought has repeatedly caused catastrophes in certain parts of Africa. In the Sahel, a grasslands region south of the Sahara Desert, there was a severe drought in the late 1960s and early 1970s. In the late 1970s, drought struck the eastern part of the continent. Thousands of people died.

Have students use the *Readers' Guide to Periodical Literature* to research the subject. Tell them the years of recent major droughts and suggest that they look in volumes that cover these times.

Have students retrieve some of the relevant articles identified by the *Guide.* As they read, have them look for the answers to the following questions:

- What physical and geographic factors cause droughts?
- Why do droughts in some areas result in such severe famines?
- If a person manages to survive a famine, what may be the long-term effects on him or her?
- What can be done to avert such tragic situations in the future?
- What can the world community do to alleviate the problem of drought?

The Sahel

A Time Line of African Independence

I n order to improve students' grasp of the history of modern Africa, have them make time lines of the important dates in the struggle for independence by the native peoples of the continent. They can begin by using an almanac or other reference book to identify the year in which each African nation achieved independence. For certain years, such as 1960, it is impressive to list all the nations that became independent!

Have students research, in small groups, the history of each nation's struggle for independence. Encourage students to add their findings to the time line.

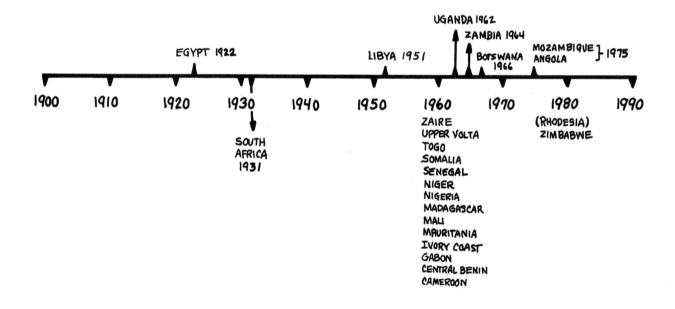

Africa's Animals and Plants

Have students use nature guides, travel guides, and basic geography books to create a bulletin board display of Africa's many unusual plants and animals. First, have students form groups to research the animals and the plant life of specific regions such as tropical rain forest, grasslands, desert, highlands. Some animals to research include the following:

cheetah	rhinoceros	hartebeest	wart hog
Grant's gazelle	baboon	hyena	chimpanzee
antelope	zebra	jackal	anteater
impala	hippopotamus	ostrich	Thomson's gazelle
lion	leopard	crocodile	
elephant	giraffe	wildebeest	

Suggest that students condense the information they find so that it will fit on index cards. The cards can be accompanied by pictures, either drawn or cut out from old magazines.

Next, have some students prepare a map of Africa with the various regions clearly indicated.

Finally, have volunteers form a coordinating committee for the project. Have them decide how the researchers' work is to be displayed and coordinated with the map. Suggest that they set a size limit for pictures and map out a spot for every researcher's work.

CHEETAH   ZEBRA   WILDEBEEST   OSTRICH

African Textile Designs

Africa is known for its textiles. Many African peoples weave cloth in beautiful patterns, using a variety of threads. Others print their cloth by hand with elaborate designs.

Show students some samples of African textile designs, prints in particular. Then have the class print their own scarves using African motifs.

For this project you will need wooden blocks, an old inner tube or large piece of thick felt, glue, several colors of textile paint (available at craft stores—be sure to use nontoxic paint), and large squares of cloth in bright colors.

Have students draw a motif no larger than the size of a wooden block, which they can repeat all over a piece of material to make a scarf or wall hanging. Have them look at pictures of African textiles for ideas. Then have them cut their design out of the rubber or felt and glue it securely to one side of the wooden block. (Note: rubber stamps can be rinsed and reused.)

Have them empty the textile paints into small flat dishes, thinning them a little with water if necessary. To print, have students dip their blocks into the ink and press onto the cloth. The paint will air-dry in a couple of hours.

Part of a fabric made of millions of tiny beads, this braided design is typical of Nigeria.

This Nigerian fabric uses figures from Yoruba folklore and mythology.

The design of this Hausa robe is based on removing small bits of fabric according to a regular pattern.

Answers to "Countries, Cities, and Natural Features of Africa," page 94: **1.** c, s **2.** f, t **3.** g, r **4.** e, l **5.** h, n **6.** j, k **7.** a, p **8.** b, m **9.** i, o **10.** d, q

Answers to "Natural Resources of Africa," page 95: **1.** the Sahara Desert and the western coast of Nigeria and Angola **2.** gold, coal, diamonds, antimony, manganese, copper, iron **3.** Zaire **4.** along the Mediterranean coast, in the southern part of the continent, and along the Nile **5.** Zaire, the areas around Africa's large lakes, and along the western coast of Africa **6.** the southern part of the continent, the Mediterranean coast, and the Nile Valley

Countries, Cities, and Natural Features of Africa

Match each country with a city and a natural feature. Use the encyclopedia and other books to find the answers.

1. Zaire   _____ _____

2. South Africa   _____ _____

3. Libya   _____ _____

4. Morocco   _____ _____

5. Tanzania   _____ _____

6. Ghana   _____ _____

7. Kenya   _____ _____

8. Egypt   _____ _____

9. Madagascar   _____ _____

10. Zimbabwe   _____ _____

a. Nairobi

b. Cairo

c. Kinshasa

d. Salisbury

e. Casablanca

f. Cape Town

g. Tripoli

h. Dar es Salaam

i. Antananarivo

j. Accra

k. world's largest producer of cocoa

l. Atlas Mountains

m. a fertile delta

n. highest and lowest points in Africa

o. an island

p. home of Masai Mara and other game preserves

q. borders spectacular waterfall

r. desert; large oil reserves

s. tropical rain forests; beginning of one of Africa's longest rivers

t. plentiful gold, diamonds, and coal

Name _____ Date _____

Natural Resources of Africa

Use the resource maps below to answer the questions.

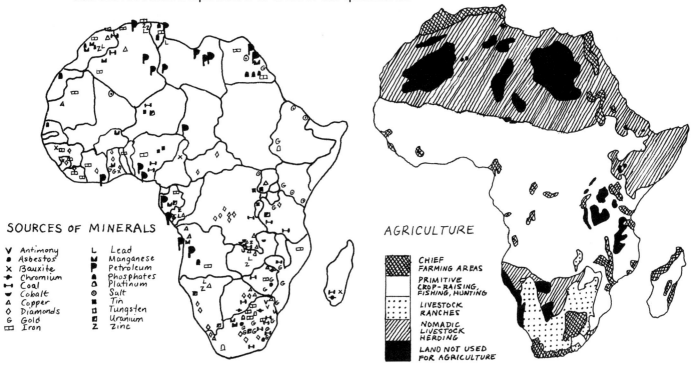

SOURCES OF MINERALS

V	Antimony	L	Lead
●	Asbestos	M	Manganese
X	Bauxite	P	Petroleum
✦	Chromium	▲	Phosphates
H	Coal	◭	Platinum
⏷	Cobalt	⊙	Salt
△	Copper	■	Tin
◇	Diamonds	⬚	Tungsten
G	Gold	⬓	Uranium
⊞	Iron	Z	Zinc

AGRICULTURE

CHIEF FARMING AREAS

PRIMITIVE CROP-RAISING, FISHING, HUNTING

LIVESTOCK RANCHES

NOMADIC LIVESTOCK HERDING

LAND NOT USED FOR AGRICULTURE

1. What two areas have plentiful reserves of petroleum?

_____

2. South Africa has many plentiful mineral supplies. What are some of the minerals found there?

_____

3. What central African nation has many diamond mines?

_____

4. Where in Africa do you think modern farming methods are used most?

_____

5. What areas are rich in mineral resources but do not have highly developed agriculture?

_____

6. What areas are both rich in mineral resources and have well-developed agriculture?

_____

95

Reviewing Africa

Developing Nations

Discuss with students the various ways African nations are developing economically. Have each student select a country, and then use an encyclopedia or other reference books to answer the following questions with respect to the country:

- What raw materials, agricultural products, and manufactured goods is your country known for today?
- How has the country's production increased or changed focus in recent years?
- What are the reasons for this increase or shift in focus?

Have each student report briefly on his or her country. Use these reports as a basis for drawing conclusions about Africa's contributions to the world economy and the reasons why the amounts and kinds of contributions have been changing.

Exciting Tours

Have students plan an imaginary one-week tour of Africa. It need encompass only a part of the continent—but include scenic sites, places of historical interest, and important cities. The itinerary should cover more than one country. Have them include with their tour package advice to the traveler as to what sort of weather to expect, languages spoken, and customs that should be respected. In addition to reference books, students may want to use brochures from travel agents.

African Folklore

Storytelling is a strong part of African traditions. Have each student find an African folk tale and retell it orally for the class. Explain that they should use their voices and hands and choice of details to dramatize their stories and make them come alive for listeners. You may wish to introduce the topic of African folklore by reading from one of the following books, which you can later recommend to students:

Appiah, Peggy. *Tales of an Ashanti Father*. Beacon Press, 1989.

Bryan, Ashley. *Lion and the Ostrich Chicks and Other African Folk Tales.* Atheneum, 1986.